Digital Asset Custody:
Securely Managing the Future of Value

DANIEL LOCKE

DEDICATION

To my beloved family,

This book is dedicated to you, the pillars of love and support in my life. Your unwavering encouragement and understanding have been the foundation upon which I have built this work. Your patience, understanding, and belief in me have been my guiding light, and I am forever grateful for the love and strength you have bestowed upon me.

Thank you for being my constant source of inspiration and for always standing by me through every endeavor. This book is a testament to the bond we share, and I dedicate it to you with all my heart.

With love and gratitude,
Daniel

CONTENTS

ACKNOWLEDGMENTS

I would like to express my deepest gratitude to all those who have contributed to the realization of this book. First and foremost, I am immensely thankful to my family for their unwavering support, understanding, and patience throughout the process of writing this book. Their encouragement has been a constant source of inspiration.

I extend my heartfelt appreciation to my colleagues and mentors for their valuable insights, guidance, and encouragement. Their expertise and wisdom have enriched this work immeasurably.

I am also indebted to the professionals and experts in the field of digital asset custody, whose knowledge and expertise have been instrumental in shaping the content of this book.

Special thanks to the readers and reviewers who provided feedback, suggestions, and encouragement, helping to refine and improve the quality of this book.

Thank you to all who have contributed to this project in various ways. Your support has been invaluable and deeply appreciated.

1. Understanding Digital Assets

1.1 Introduction to Digital Assets

In today's interconnected world, digital assets have emerged as a disruptive force, transforming various industries and revolutionizing the way we perceive and interact with value. From cryptocurrencies like Bitcoin and Ethereum to digital tokens and non-fungible tokens (NFTs), the realm of digital assets is expanding rapidly, challenging traditional notions of ownership, finance,   and commerce. This section, "Introduction to Digital Assets," provides a comprehensive overview of digital assets, their characteristics, and their impact on the digital economy.

Digital assets, as the name suggests, are intangible assets that exist solely in electronic form. Unlike physical assets such as cash or real estate, digital assets are stored and transferred electronically, utilizing cryptographic techniques and decentralized networks for security and verification. These assets can take various forms, each with its unique features and potential applications. From currencies and tokens that facilitate transactions to digital representations of real-world assets or collectibles, digital assets encompass a wide range of possibilities.

One of the key driving factors behind the rise of digital assets is the advent of blockchain technology. Blockchain, a distributed ledger technology, provides the underlying infrastructure for many digital assets, enabling secure and transparent record-keeping. This decentralized system allows participants to interact directly with one another, removing the need for intermediaries and providing greater autonomy and control over assets.

Cryptocurrencies, perhaps the most well-known category of digital assets, have gained significant attention and adoption over the years. Bitcoin, introduced in 2009, was the first decentralized cryptocurrency, designed to enable peer-to-peer electronic transactions without the need for intermediaries. Since then, thousands of cryptocurrencies have emerged, each with its unique features and use cases. These cryptocurrencies, often powered by blockchain technology, offer benefits such as transparency, security, and accessibility, challenging traditional financial systems and monetary policies.

In addition to cryptocurrencies, digital tokens have also gained prominence in recent years. Digital tokens represent ownership or access rights to specific assets or services and are often issued through initial coin offerings (ICOs) or tokenization processes. These tokens can represent anything from company shares and utility tokens to rights to intellectual property or participation in decentralized applications (DApps). With programmability and interoperability, digital tokens enable innovative use cases, such as decentralized finance (DeFi), supply chain management, and digital identity solutions.

Non-fungible tokens (NFTs) have garnered significant attention and have become a prominent category within digital assets. NFTs represent unique and indivisible digital assets, certifying ownership and authenticity on the blockchain. These tokens have found applications in digital art, virtual real estate, gaming, and collectibles. With NFTs, creators and artists can tokenize their work, establishing verifiable ownership and creating new avenues for monetization.

The impact of digital assets extends far beyond their technological aspects. They have the potential to reshape traditional financial systems, democratize access to financial services, and foster new economic models. Digital assets facilitate borderless transactions, enabling individuals from different corners of the world to engage in financial activities with ease. Additionally, they provide opportunities for financial inclusion, empowering the unbanked and underbanked populations to access financial services and participate in global markets.

As digital assets continue to gain traction, it is important to understand their implications, benefits, and challenges. The decentralized and borderless nature of digital assets brings new considerations for security, privacy, and regulatory frameworks. Custodianship of digital assets becomes crucial, ensuring the safe storage, management, and transference of these intangible assets. The next sections of this chapter will delve deeper into the various types of digital assets, their underlying technologies, and the transformative potential they hold for the digital economy.

1.2 The Evolution of Digital Assets

Digital assets have undergone a fascinating evolution, transforming from a concept to a significant force within the global economy. Understanding this evolution is crucial to comprehending the current landscape and the potential future trajectories of digital assets. In this section, we will explore the key milestones and developments that have shaped the evolution of digital assets, from their humble beginnings to their current prominence.

The concept of digital assets can be traced back to the early days of the internet when the digitization of information started to gain momentum. As content and media transitioned from physical forms to digital files, the notion of intangible assets began to take shape. Initially, digital assets were primarily limited to digital files, such as documents, images, and multimedia. However, the scope of digital assets expanded rapidly as technology advanced and new possibilities emerged.

The introduction of cryptocurrencies in 2009 marked a significant milestone in the evolution of digital assets. Bitcoin, created by an anonymous individual or group known as Satoshi Nakamoto, introduced the concept of a decentralized, peer-to-peer digital currency. Bitcoin's underlying technology, blockchain, provided a transparent and secure system for recording transactions, challenging the traditional centralized financial systems.

Bitcoin's success paved the way for the emergence of thousands of alternative cryptocurrencies, each with its unique features and purposes. Ethereum, launched in 2015, introduced the concept of smart contracts, programmable agreements that automatically execute predefined conditions when certain criteria are met. This innovation opened up a wide range of possibilities beyond simple currency transfers, enabling the creation of decentralized applications (DApps) and the issuance of digital tokens.

The proliferation of digital tokens became a significant development in the evolution of digital assets. Digital tokens represent various assets or rights and are often issued through initial coin offerings (ICOs) or tokenization processes. These tokens can represent ownership shares in a company, access rights to a specific service or platform, or even physical assets like real estate or commodities. The tokenization of assets provides increased liquidity, fractional ownership, and opens up new investment opportunities.

Another notable development in the evolution of digital assets is the rise of non-fungible tokens (NFTs). NFTs represent unique digital assets that cannot be replicated or interchanged. This uniqueness is achieved through the use of blockchain technology, which certifies ownership and authenticity. NFTs have gained significant attention in recent years, particularly in the domains of digital art, collectibles, and virtual assets. Artists can now tokenize their work, creating a new market for digital art and providing a secure mechanism for provenance and ownership verification.

As digital assets evolved, so did the underlying technologies that support them. Blockchain technology, the backbone of many digital assets, has undergone significant advancements and variations. The introduction of different consensus mechanisms, such as proof of stake (PoS) and delegated proof of stake (DPoS), addressed scalability and energy consumption concerns associated with traditional proof of work (PoW) mechanisms.

Interoperability between different blockchain networks and protocols has also become a focal point in the evolution of digital assets. Projects like Polkadot, Cosmos, and interoperability protocols like Inter-Blockchain Communication

(IBC) aim to connect disparate blockchain networks, enabling the seamless transfer of assets and information across different ecosystems. This interoperability fosters collaboration, expands use cases, and enhances the overall utility of digital assets.

Moreover, advancements in decentralized finance (DeFi) have propelled the adoption and utility of digital assets. DeFi protocols leverage smart contracts and blockchain technology to enable financial services such as lending, borrowing, and decentralized exchanges without the need for intermediaries. This innovation has democratized access to financial services, providing individuals worldwide with opportunities to participate in financial activities traditionally reserved for a select few.

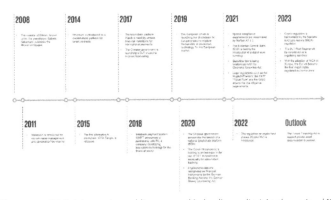

Source: KPMG report on Digital Assets. https://kpmg.com/de/en/home/insights/overview/digital-assets.html

Looking ahead, the evolution of digital assets shows no signs of slowing down. As technological innovations continue to emerge and regulatory frameworks evolve, digital assets are poised to further disrupt traditional industries and redefine the way we perceive and interact with value. The potential applications extend beyond finance, with digital assets finding utility in areas such as supply chain management, healthcare, identity verification, and more.

Understanding the evolution of digital assets provides valuable insights into their current state and future potential. By grasping the historical context and the milestones along the way, we can appreciate the transformative power of digital assets and the possibilities they unlock. The subsequent sections will delve deeper into the different types and categories of digital assets, exploring their unique characteristics, use cases, and the challenges and opportunities they present in the modern digital economy.

1.3 Types and Categories of Digital Assets

Digital assets encompass a diverse range of intangible assets that exist solely in electronic form, each with its unique characteristics and use cases. Understanding the various types and categories of digital assets is crucial for navigating the complex landscape of the digital economy. In this section, we will explore the different classifications of digital assets, shedding light on their defining features and potential applications.

Based on structure, characteristics and usage, six types of digital assets exist:

Cryptocurrencies: The Pioneers of Digital Assets

Cryptocurrencies, such as Bitcoin, Ethereum, and Litecoin, are among the earliest and most well-known types of digital assets. These currencies are decentralized digital representations of value that utilize cryptographic techniques to secure transactions and control the creation of new units. Cryptocurrencies typically operate on blockchain networks, ensuring transparency and immutability.

Bitcoin, introduced in 2009, was the first decentralized cryptocurrency, designed to enable peer-to-peer electronic transactions without the need for intermediaries. It serves as a store of value and a medium of exchange, providing users with greater financial autonomy and security. Bitcoin's success paved the way for the emergence of numerous alternative cryptocurrencies, collectively known as altcoins.

Ethereum, launched in 2015, introduced the concept of programmable smart contracts, enabling the creation of decentralized applications (DApps) and facilitating the issuance of digital tokens. This programmability expanded the potential use cases of cryptocurrencies beyond simple transactions, enabling developers to build decentralized platforms and services on top of the Ethereum blockchain.

Cryptocurrencies are a new breed of money that operate independently of any central authority, be it a bank or government. These ingenious currencies are governed by a public ledger known as the blockchain, which records and cryptographically secures all transactions. Since they run on a distributed network, there is no central authority to oversee or issue them, rendering them impervious to government interference. Cryptocurrencies can be acquired through mining, purchased via cryptocurrency exchanges, or earned as rewards on the blockchain network. They are a fantastic choice for making payments or investing. Among the most prominent cryptocurrencies are Ethereum, Bitcoin, and Litecoin.

Let delve into the main features of these digital wonders:

- Decentralized - Cryptocurrencies operate on a distributed network, which means that there is no central authority to oversee them. Instead, they are governed by a public ledger called the blockchain.
- Anonymous - Cryptocurrencies offer a degree of anonymity that traditional money does not. Transactions are recorded on the blockchain, but the identities of those involved are kept private.
- Volatile - The value of cryptocurrencies can fluctuate wildly over short periods, making them a high-risk investment.
- Secure - Cryptocurrencies are secured by cryptography, making them difficult to counterfeit or hack. Transactions on the blockchain are immutable and cannot be altered once recorded.

Digital Tokens: Unlocking New Possibilities

Digital tokens represent a broader category of digital assets that can represent ownership rights, access to services, or other forms of value. These tokens can be issued and managed on blockchain platforms, allowing for increased transparency and liquidity.

Utility tokens, also known as app coins or user tokens, provide access to specific products or services within a decentralized application. These tokens enable participation in the network and grant users certain rights or privileges. For example, within a decentralized social media platform, utility tokens might be required to access premium features or reward content creators.

Security tokens, on the other hand, represent ownership rights to underlying assets, such as equity in a company, real estate, or investment funds. These tokens are subject to securities regulations and provide investors with the opportunity to participate in traditionally illiquid assets in a more accessible and efficient manner. Security tokens enable fractional ownership, increased liquidity, and streamlined transferability.

Stablecoins, a type of digital token, are designed to minimize price volatility and maintain a stable value relative to a specific asset, such as a fiat currency or a commodity. Stablecoins provide stability and serve as a bridge between the traditional financial system and the decentralized digital economy. They enable users to retain the advantages of cryptocurrencies while minimizing exposure to price fluctuations.

These assets have been tokenized on the blockchain of an existing cryptocurrency, and though they share similarities with cryptocurrencies, they are a separate asset class. Tokens can be traded via a blockchain, but they can also represent more traditional assets like real estate or art.

Now, let's delve into the main features of these fascinating tokens:

- Permissionless - Tokens operate on a permissionless blockchain, which means that anyone with an internet connection can participate in the network. There is no need for intermediaries or gatekeepers, making it easy for anyone to use.
- Transparent - Transactions involving tokens are transparent and open for anyone to see. This transparency ensures that there is no room for fraudulent activities or scams.
- Trustless - Tokens operate on a trustless blockchain, which means that there is no need for trust between parties. Transactions are secured by the blockchain's consensus mechanism, ensuring that they are valid and cannot be tampered with.

Non-Fungible Tokens (NFTs): Uniqueness in the Digital Realm

Non-fungible tokens (NFTs) represent a unique subset of digital assets, certifying the ownership and authenticity of digital artifacts, collectibles, and intellectual property. Unlike cryptocurrencies and other digital tokens, which are fungible and interchangeable, each NFT is distinct and cannot be replicated.

NFTs have gained significant attention and adoption in recent years, particularly in the domains of digital art, virtual real estate, gaming, and collectibles. Artists and creators can tokenize their work, establishing verifiable ownership, provenance, and scarcity in the digital realm. NFTs enable new monetization models and provide a secure mechanism for creators to sell and trade their digital assets.

The rise of NFTs has opened up a wide range of possibilities, allowing individuals to own and trade unique digital assets, ranging from artwork and music to virtual real estate and in-game items. With NFTs, creators and collectors can engage in a new form of digital ownership and establish a direct connection between creators and consumers.

These tokens are unique digital content linked to the blockchain, much like the technology used for cryptocurrencies. Unlike fungible tokens, which can be exchanged for other tokens of equal value, non-fungible tokens are one-of-a-kind and cannot be replaced or exchanged with another identical asset. They serve as certificates of ownership for digital assets, providing authentication to prove their authenticity. NFTs are especially popular among artists who sell their digital art and media recordings, as they offer ownership rights and enable creators to protect their work.

Let explore the main features of these fascinating tokens:
- Defines ownership rights - NFTs provide proof of ownership for digital assets, allowing creators to retain control over their work and receive compensation for its use.
- Unique - Each NFT is one-of-a-kind and cannot be replicated or replaced with another asset of equal value. This feature makes them highly valuable and sought after.
- Irreplaceable - As mentioned earlier, NFTs are unique and cannot be exchanged for other tokens of equal value. This feature ensures that each NFT is truly one-of-a-kind.
- Extensible - NFTs can be combined with each other to create new, more complex tokens. This feature allows for endless possibilities in the world of digital art and media.

Stablecoins: Embracing the Stability

Let's introduce the latest innovation in the world of cryptocurrencies: stablecoins. These digital currencies are tethered to another currency, commodity, or financial instrument to maintain stability and minimize price volatility. As a result, stablecoins offer a less volatile alternative to traditional cryptocurrencies like Bitcoin and Ethereum. They are ideal for cross-border payments and transfers at a lower fee, making them an excellent optional payment method for products and services.

Now, let's delve into the main features of these fascinating stablecoins:
- Stable - Stablecoins offer a stable value due to their connection to another currency, commodity, or financial instrument. This feature ensures that they maintain their value over time.
- Transparent - Transactions involving stablecoins are transparent and open for anyone to see. This transparency ensures that there is no room for fraudulent activities or scams.
- Decentralized - Stablecoins operate on a decentralized blockchain, which means that there is no central authority overseeing them. Instead, they are governed by a public ledger called the blockchain.

CBDC: virtual money backed and issued by a central bank.

Central Bank Digital Currency (CBDC) is a novel form of digital currency that has been authorized by central banks and is intrinsically linked to the value of the fiat currency of the issuing nation. Unlike decentralized cryptocurrencies such as Bitcoin and Ethereum, CBDCs have a distinct set of advantages. They are designed to facilitate faster and more efficient payments, increase financial inclusion, and provide central banks with more effective monetary policy tools.

The Digital Yuan, which was created by the People's Bank of China, is a noteworthy example of a CBDC that has been launched to enhance the financial inclusion and stability of the nation.

CBDCs have several key features that make them stand out. For instance, they have low transaction costs and enable speedy transactions. These attributes make them an attractive option for individuals and businesses alike who are looking for a more seamless and cost-effective way to conduct transactions.

Digital Bonds: The bonds of the future

A bond is a financial instrument utilized by borrowers, be it corporations or governments, to secure capital. The borrowed amount is then repaid, along with interest, over a fixed period of time.

Digital bonds resemble traditional bond offerings as they aim to provide a low-risk and low-return investment opportunity. However, the fascinating twist lies in the fact that the entire process of issuing, trading, and settling digital bonds takes place online through the blockchain. This ingenious functionality ensures a streamlined and efficient process when compared to its traditional counterparts, resulting in quicker transactions and cost savings.

In summary, the key features of digital bonds are their efficiency, reliability, and verifiability. They offer a modern and technologically advanced approach to bond investments.

The Role of Blockchain Technology in Digital Assets

Blockchain technology serves as the underlying infrastructure for many digital assets, providing transparency, security, and immutability. Blockchain networks operate on distributed ledger technology, where multiple nodes in a network verify and validate transactions. This decentralized consensus mechanism ensures the integrity of digital assets, preventing double-spending and unauthorized modifications.

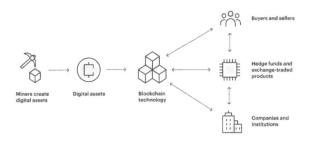

Blockchain Technology in Digital Assets

Blockchain networks offer various advantages for digital assets, including transparency, auditability, and resilience. Each transaction is recorded on the blockchain, creating an immutable trail of ownership and transaction history. Participants can verify the authenticity and provenance of digital assets, enhancing trust and reducing the risk of fraud.

Furthermore, blockchain technology enables peer-to-peer transactions, removing the need for intermediaries. This disintermediation reduces costs, streamlines processes, and provides individuals with greater control over their digital assets. Blockchain networks also facilitate global accessibility, allowing users to engage in cross-border transactions with ease and efficiency.

Conclusion

Understanding the types and categories of digital assets is essential for comprehending the diverse landscape of the digital economy. From cryptocurrencies to digital tokens and non-fungible tokens (NFTs), digital assets offer new possibilities for value creation, ownership, and participation. Blockchain technology serves as the backbone of many digital assets, providing security, transparency, and decentralization.

As the digital asset ecosystem continues to evolve, new types of assets and innovative use cases will undoubtedly emerge. This rapidly changing landscape presents both challenges and opportunities, requiring individuals, institutions, and policymakers to adapt and navigate this dynamic digital frontier. In the subsequent sections, we will explore the role of blockchain technology, delve deeper into the features and functions of digital assets, and examine the challenges and considerations involved in their secure custody.

1.4 Cryptocurrencies: The Pioneers of Digital Assets

Cryptocurrencies have emerged as the pioneers and trailblazers of the digital asset landscape, revolutionizing the way we perceive and interact with value. In this section, we will delve into the world of cryptocurrencies, exploring their origins, underlying technology, and the transformative impact they have had on the financial industry and beyond. Cryptocurrencies are decentralized digital currencies that utilize cryptographic techniques to secure transactions, control the creation of new units, and ensure the integrity of the underlying ledger. The advent of Bitcoin in 2009 marked the birth of the first decentralized cryptocurrency, created by the enigmatic Satoshi Nakamoto. Bitcoin introduced the concept of a peer-to-peer electronic cash system, enabling users to transact directly with one another without the need for intermediaries.

The underlying technology that powers cryptocurrencies is blockchain, a distributed ledger system that records all transactions in a transparent and immutable manner. Blockchain ensures that every transaction is validated by a network of participants, eliminating the need for a central authority or trusted intermediary. This decentralization, combined with the cryptographic security measures, provides unprecedented transparency, security, and trust in the digital realm.

Bitcoin's success as the first decentralized cryptocurrency paved the way for the proliferation of thousands of alternative cryptocurrencies, often referred to as altcoins. Each altcoin possesses its unique features, use cases, and underlying technologies. Ethereum, launched in 2015, introduced a groundbreaking innovation with the concept of smart contracts. Smart contracts are self-executing agreements with predefined conditions coded into the blockchain. This programmability allows for the creation of decentralized applications (DApps) and the issuance of digital tokens, opening up a world of possibilities beyond simple currency transactions.

The impact of cryptocurrencies extends far beyond their use as a medium of exchange or a store of value. Cryptocurrencies have challenged traditional financial systems, enabling individuals to transact across borders without the need for intermediaries or centralized control. These digital currencies provide financial autonomy, privacy, and security, particularly in regions with unstable or restrictive financial infrastructures.

Moreover, cryptocurrencies have fostered a sense of community and participation through the concept of mining and staking. Miners contribute computing power to the network, validating and adding transactions to the blockchain while being rewarded with newly minted cryptocurrency units. This consensus mechanism not only secures the network but also allows individuals to actively participate in the creation and governance of cryptocurrencies.

Cryptocurrencies have also gained significant attention as investment assets. The volatility and potential for significant returns have attracted investors seeking to diversify their portfolios and capitalize on the emerging digital economy. The rise of cryptocurrency exchanges and trading platforms has made it easier than ever for individuals to buy, sell, and trade cryptocurrencies, further fueling their popularity and liquidity.

In addition to their financial impact, cryptocurrencies have sparked technological innovations and disruptive business models. Blockchain technology, the foundation of cryptocurrencies, has found applications in various industries beyond finance. It has the potential to streamline supply chain management, enhance data security, and improve governance processes. The decentralized and transparent nature of blockchain technology is reshaping how businesses and organizations operate, creating new opportunities for efficiency, trust, and collaboration.

However, cryptocurrencies are not without challenges and considerations. Their volatility and regulatory uncertainties present risks for investors and businesses alike. The potential for fraudulent activities, security breaches, and the illicit use of cryptocurrencies necessitates robust security measures, regulatory frameworks, and industry standards. Balancing innovation and risk mitigation is essential to foster the long-term sustainability and acceptance of cryptocurrencies.

In conclusion, cryptocurrencies have played a pioneering role in the digital asset landscape, revolutionizing the way we perceive and transact value. Their decentralized nature, cryptographic security, and potential for innovation have made them a disruptive force in finance and beyond. As cryptocurrencies continue to evolve and mature, their impact on the global economy and the transformation of traditional industries is likely to accelerate. Understanding the fundamentals of cryptocurrencies and their underlying technologies is crucial for individuals, businesses, and policymakers seeking to navigate the dynamic and evolving digital asset landscape.

1.5 Digital Tokens: Unlocking New Possibilities

Digital tokens represent a dynamic and versatile category of digital assets that have gained significant attention and adoption in recent years. These tokens, built on blockchain technology, offer unique functionalities and serve various purposes, ranging from access to services and platforms to ownership rights and beyond. In this section, we will delve into the world of digital tokens, exploring their characteristics, use cases, and the transformative potential they hold in the digital economy.

Digital tokens are programmable units of value that can be created, managed, and transacted on a blockchain network. These tokens leverage the underlying infrastructure of blockchain technology, ensuring transparency, security, and decentralized governance. They provide a means of representing and transferring both tangible and intangible assets in a digital format, enabling increased liquidity, fractional ownership, and innovative business models.

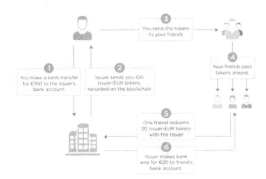

How do asset-backed tokens work?

One prominent category of digital tokens is utility tokens, also known as app coins or user tokens. Utility tokens are designed to provide access to specific products, services, or features within a decentralized application (DApp) or platform. They represent a form of digital currency that enables users to interact with the underlying ecosystem. By owning utility tokens, users can unlock functionalities, participate in platform governance, and enjoy various benefits within the decentralized network.

The utility token model has gained significant popularity, particularly in the realm of decentralized finance (DeFi). DeFi platforms leverage smart contracts and utility tokens to provide a range of financial services, including lending, borrowing, decentralized exchanges, and yield farming. Utility tokens play a crucial role in these ecosystems, providing users with voting rights, fee discounts, or access to exclusive services.

Another category of digital tokens is security tokens, which represent ownership rights to underlying assets, such as equity in a company, real estate, investment funds, or other financial instruments. Security tokens are subject to regulatory frameworks and securities laws, offering a compliant and regulated approach to digital ownership. By digitizing traditional assets, security tokens enable fractional ownership, increased liquidity, and streamlined transferability, opening up new investment opportunities for a broader range of investors.

Stablecoins represent yet another significant category of digital tokens. These tokens are designed to maintain a stable value relative to a specific asset, such as a fiat currency or a commodity. Stablecoins address the volatility concerns often associated with other cryptocurrencies, allowing users to transact and store value with minimal price fluctuations. The stability of stablecoins makes them suitable for various use cases, including remittances, e-commerce, and as a unit of account within decentralized applications.

Nonetheless, the versatility of digital tokens extends beyond these categories. Tokens can represent a wide array of assets, such as real estate properties, artwork, intellectual property rights, or even loyalty points within a specific ecosystem. By tokenizing these assets, the ownership and transfer of value become more efficient, transparent, and accessible to a global audience.

The tokenization of assets holds transformative potential across industries. For instance, real estate tokenization allows for the fractional ownership of properties, making real estate investments more accessible and liquid. Similarly, art tokenization enables fractional ownership of artworks, democratizing access to art investments and supporting artists by providing new avenues for monetization.

Digital tokens also enable innovative fundraising models through initial coin offerings (ICOs) or token sales. By issuing tokens, projects and startups can raise capital directly from a global pool of investors, bypassing traditional funding channels. This decentralized crowdfunding mechanism has revolutionized early-stage funding and has allowed innovative ideas to come to fruition.

The advent of digital tokens has transformed the concept of ownership, value exchange, and participation in digital ecosystems. By leveraging blockchain technology, digital tokens provide verifiable scarcity, provenance, and secure ownership rights. They unlock new possibilities for economic models, incentive structures, and collaboration.

However, the growing popularity and adoption of digital tokens have also given rise to challenges and considerations. Regulatory frameworks and compliance requirements vary across jurisdictions, necessitating careful navigation to ensure legal compliance. Security and custody solutions must be robust to safeguard digital tokens from theft or unauthorized access. Additionally, interoperability between different blockchain networks and token standards is crucial for the seamless transfer and exchange of digital tokens.

If we look at the industry, for the first time, there is a combination of central bank funds' safety and institutional quality with blockchain technology's innovative functionality and resilience. Why does this matter? Tokenization allows fast, secure, and automated execution of business and financial processes with lower transaction costs and risks.

In conclusion, digital tokens represent a versatile and transformative category of digital assets, enabling unique functionalities and use cases. Utility tokens, security tokens, stablecoins, and asset-backed tokens offer opportunities for access, ownership, and value exchange within decentralized ecosystems. The tokenization of assets has the potential to disrupt traditional industries, democratize access to investments, and foster new economic models. By understanding the characteristics and possibilities of digital tokens, individuals and businesses can leverage their potential and participate in the evolving digital economy.

1.6 Non-Fungible Tokens (NFTs): Uniqueness in the Digital Realm

Non-fungible tokens (NFTs) have taken the digital world by storm, introducing a new paradigm of ownership and uniqueness in the realm of digital assets. These tokens represent one-of-a-kind digital items, whether it be art, collectibles, virtual real estate, or even in-game items. In this section, we will explore the concept of non-fungible tokens, their underlying technology, and the impact they have had on various industries.

At their core, non-fungible tokens are digital assets that are indivisible and unique. Unlike cryptocurrencies or other digital tokens that are interchangeable on a one-to-one basis, each NFT has distinct characteristics and properties that set it apart from any other token. This uniqueness is made possible through blockchain technology, which provides a decentralized and transparent ledger to verify the authenticity, ownership, and provenance of these digital assets.

The advent of NFTs has unlocked new possibilities for creators, artists, and collectors. Artists can tokenize their digital creations, including artwork, music, videos, and more, establishing verifiable ownership and scarcity in the digital realm. This has created new avenues for artists to monetize their work and gain recognition, as well as enabling a direct connection between creators and consumers. With NFTs, the ownership of digital art can be easily transferred and tracked, eliminating issues of copyright infringement and establishing a sustainable framework for artists in the digital age.

Beyond art, NFTs have extended their reach into the world of collectibles. Digital collectibles, or crypto-collectibles, encompass a wide range of items, such as virtual trading cards, virtual pets, and virtual real estate. These digital collectibles leverage the uniqueness and scarcity provided by NFTs to create a thriving marketplace for enthusiasts and collectors. The ownership of these digital collectibles can be easily proven, and the value is determined by factors such as rarity, demand, and historical significance.

Larva Labs, 9 Cryptopunks, 2021. Courtesy Christie's

Virtual real estate is another emerging field within the NFT space. With the advent of virtual worlds and metaverses, individuals and businesses can own and trade virtual land, buildings, and other digital assets within these virtual environments. NFTs serve as the foundation for establishing ownership rights and enabling transactions in these virtual realms. Virtual real estate provides opportunities for creativity, social interaction, and even potential economic activities within the digital landscape.

Gaming is yet another sector that has been significantly impacted by the introduction of NFTs. In-game items, character skins, and virtual accessories can now be tokenized as NFTs, allowing players to truly own and trade their digital possessions. This introduces a new level of value and scarcity to the gaming experience, as players can buy, sell, and collect rare and unique in-game items. The integration of NFTs into gaming ecosystems provides economic opportunities for players and developers alike, fostering a vibrant and decentralized gaming economy.

The implications of NFTs extend beyond the realm of art, collectibles, virtual real estate, and gaming. NFTs can be applied to various domains, including intellectual property rights, digital identity, and supply chain management. By tokenizing these assets and records, individuals and businesses can establish verifiable ownership, enhance transparency, and streamline processes. For example, NFTs can be used to track the authenticity and ownership of luxury goods, ensuring the legitimacy of high-value items.

While the rise of NFTs has unlocked tremendous potential, it is important to address certain considerations and challenges. Environmental concerns regarding the energy consumption associated with certain blockchain networks, particularly those utilizing proof-of-work consensus mechanisms, have garnered attention. It is crucial for the industry to explore more sustainable alternatives, such as transitioning to energy-efficient consensus algorithms like proof of stake.

Additionally, the NFT space has witnessed instances of copyright infringement and unauthorized use of intellectual property. It is essential to establish guidelines, best practices, and legal frameworks to protect the rights of creators and ensure ethical practices within the industry. Education and awareness play a crucial role in fostering a responsible and sustainable NFT ecosystem.

In conclusion, non-fungible tokens have introduced a paradigm shift in the digital asset landscape, enabling verifiable uniqueness, ownership, and value in the digital realm. Through the power of blockchain technology, NFTs have transformed the art market, collectibles industry, gaming ecosystems, and beyond. They have provided creators with new monetization opportunities, collectors with new avenues for ownership, and individuals with increased access to digital assets. As the potential of NFTs continues to unfold, it is important to strike a balance between innovation, responsible practices, and the preservation of integrity and authenticity within the digital asset landscape.

1.7 The Impact of Blockchain on Digital Asset Custody

Blockchain technology has emerged as a transformative force in the realm of digital asset custody, revolutionizing the way assets are secured, stored, and transferred. In this section, we will explore the impact of blockchain technology on custody practices, highlighting its benefits, challenges, and potential future developments.

Traditionally, the custody of assets, especially financial instruments and valuables, relied on centralized intermediaries such as banks, custodians, and financial institutions. These intermediaries acted as trusted third parties responsible for safeguarding assets on behalf of individuals and institutions. However, this centralized custody model often posed challenges, including potential single points of failure, lack of transparency, and high costs.

Blockchain technology addresses these challenges by providing a decentralized, transparent, and secure framework for digital asset custody. At its core, blockchain is a distributed ledger that records transactions and asset ownership in a tamper-resistant and transparent manner. By utilizing consensus algorithms and cryptographic techniques, blockchain ensures the integrity and immutability of data, eliminating the need for intermediaries and establishing trust among participants.

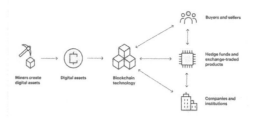

Digital assets in a Blockchain

One of the key benefits of blockchain-based custody is increased security. Blockchain's decentralized nature and cryptographic algorithms make it highly resistant to unauthorized modifications and tampering. Assets held in blockchain-based custody solutions are protected by robust encryption, making them less vulnerable to hacking or unauthorized access. Additionally, the transparent and auditable nature of blockchain transactions enhances accountability and reduces the risk of fraud.

Another advantage of blockchain-based custody is improved efficiency. Traditional custody processes often involve multiple intermediaries, leading to delays, complex workflows, and increased costs. With blockchain technology, custody processes can be streamlined and automated, reducing manual interventions and increasing operational efficiency. Smart contracts, self-executing agreements coded on the blockchain, enable automated asset transfers, ensuring seamless custody operations and faster settlement times.

Furthermore, blockchain-based custody provides enhanced transparency and auditability. Every transaction recorded on the blockchain is visible to all participants, creating a transparent and auditable record of asset movements. This level of transparency can increase trust among stakeholders and provide regulators with better visibility into custody practices. Auditing and compliance processes can be simplified, as the transaction history on the blockchain serves as an immutable source of truth.

Blockchain technology also enables fractional ownership and increased liquidity. By tokenizing assets on a blockchain, they can be divided into smaller units, allowing for fractional ownership. This fractionalization opens up investment opportunities to a broader range of investors, enabling them to participate in assets that were traditionally inaccessible due to high minimum investment requirements. Additionally, blockchain-based markets and decentralized exchanges provide liquidity, allowing for efficient trading and transferability of digital assets.

While blockchain-based custody offers numerous benefits, challenges and considerations remain. Scalability is a key challenge, as blockchain networks must handle a high volume of transactions to support widespread adoption. Efforts to improve scalability, such as layer-two solutions and interoperability protocols, are actively being explored to address this limitation.

Another challenge is the integration of blockchain-based custody solutions with existing regulatory frameworks. As custody of traditional financial instruments often falls under specific regulatory requirements, aligning blockchain-based custody practices with existing regulations can be complex. Regulators are actively working to develop frameworks that accommodate the unique characteristics of blockchain-based custody while ensuring investor protection and compliance.

Interoperability is another consideration in blockchain-based custody. As different blockchain networks and protocols emerge, ensuring seamless transferability and interoperability of assets across these networks becomes crucial. Standards and protocols that facilitate interoperability, such as atomic swaps and cross-chain bridges, are being developed to address this challenge.

Looking to the future, the potential of blockchain-based custody extends beyond financial instruments. It has the potential to disrupt other industries, including supply chain management, healthcare, intellectual property, and more. By leveraging blockchain technology, asset ownership and transfer can be streamlined, eliminating complexities and intermediaries.

In conclusion, blockchain technology has ushered in a new era of digital asset custody, offering increased security, transparency, efficiency, and liquidity. The decentralized and transparent nature of blockchain provides a robust framework for custody, minimizing the reliance on centralized intermediaries. However, challenges related to scalability, regulation, and interoperability must be addressed to fully realize the potential of blockchain-based custody. As the technology continues to evolve, blockchain-based custody has the potential to reshape how we secure and manage digital assets across industries.

1.8 Decentralization and Trust: Key Features of Digital Assets

In the realm of digital asset custody, decentralization and trust are two fundamental features that set digital assets apart from traditional financial instruments. Understanding these key characteristics is crucial for custodians and asset owners alike. In this section, we will explore the concepts of decentralization and trust as they pertain to digital assets, highlighting their significance and implications for custodial services.

Decentralization lies at the core of many digital assets, offering a paradigm shift from traditional centralized financial systems. Unlike traditional financial instruments that rely on centralized intermediaries such as banks or clearinghouses, digital assets operate on decentralized networks, typically based on blockchain technology. This decentralized nature introduces several benefits and challenges in the custody of digital assets.

One of the primary advantages of decentralization is the removal of single points of failure. In traditional financial systems, a central authority or intermediary controls the custody and transfer of assets. This centralized control creates vulnerabilities, as a breach or failure in the central authority can lead to significant disruptions or loss of assets. With decentralized digital assets, the control and ownership are distributed across a network of participants, reducing the reliance on any single entity and enhancing the resilience of the system.

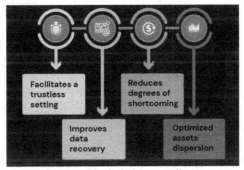

Source: Blockchain-councli.org

Decentralization also enables increased transparency and auditability. Blockchain technology, the backbone of many digital assets, provides a transparent and immutable ledger that records all transactions. This transparency allows asset owners and custodians to verify the integrity and ownership of assets in real-time. The immutability of blockchain records ensures that once a transaction is recorded, it cannot be altered, providing a high level of trust and auditability.

Trust is a foundational aspect of digital asset custody, closely tied to the concept of decentralization. In traditional financial systems, trust is largely placed in centralized intermediaries to facilitate transactions and custody assets. With digital assets, trust is distributed across the network and relies on cryptographic algorithms and consensus mechanisms to ensure the integrity and security of transactions. This distributed trust model offers unique advantages but also presents challenges for custodians.

Custodians play a vital role in building trust within the digital asset ecosystem. By offering secure and reliable custodial services, custodians instill confidence in asset owners and provide a bridge between the decentralized nature of digital assets and the need for professional custody. Custodians must demonstrate their ability to protect assets, maintain the integrity of transactions, and navigate the complexities of decentralized networks.

To effectively handle the custody of decentralized digital assets, custodians must adapt their operational processes and security measures. This includes the implementation of multi-signature schemes, where multiple authorized signatures are required to execute a transaction, reducing the risk of a single point of failure. Custodians must also carefully manage private keys, implementing robust key management practices to ensure the secure storage and use of these critical assets.

The evolving landscape of decentralized finance (DeFi) presents both opportunities and challenges for custodians. DeFi protocols leverage blockchain technology and smart contracts to offer financial services without intermediaries. While DeFi enhances financial inclusivity and accessibility, it introduces complexities for custodians in terms of custody solutions and risk management. Custodians must navigate the decentralized nature of DeFi, understanding the risks and exploring how to provide custodial services for decentralized assets effectively.

Another consideration in decentralized digital asset custody is the need for interoperability. Digital assets operate on various blockchain networks, each with its protocols and standards. Custodians must navigate the interoperability challenges to custody assets across different blockchains and ensure seamless transfers. This requires custodians to stay informed about emerging interoperability solutions, engage with industry discussions, and collaborate with other custodians and stakeholders to establish industry-wide standards and best practices.

The Global Decentralized Finance Market Size is valued at 14.10 billion in 2022 and is predicted to reach 398.77 billion by the year 2031 at a 45.16% CAGR during the forecast period for 2023-2031 (Source: Insight Ace Analytic).

Custodians operating in the decentralized digital asset space must also consider the evolving regulatory landscape. As decentralized assets gain mainstream attention, regulatory authorities are developing frameworks to ensure consumer protection, prevent financial crimes, and address potential systemic risks. Custodians must closely monitor regulatory developments, adapt their compliance programs, and engage with regulators to navigate the evolving regulatory landscape effectively.

In conclusion, decentralization and trust are key features of digital assets that significantly impact the custody landscape. Decentralization removes single points of failure, enhances transparency, and improves auditability. However, it also introduces challenges such as interoperability and regulatory considerations. Custodians play a critical role in building trust within the decentralized ecosystem, implementing robust security measures, adapting to the complexities of decentralized networks, and providing reliable custody services. By understanding and embracing the features of decentralization and trust, custodians can effectively navigate the custody of digital assets and contribute to the growth and maturity of the digital asset ecosystem.

1.9 Smart Contracts: Automating Value Exchange

Smart contracts have emerged as a revolutionary technology in the world of digital assets, enabling the automation and execution of complex transactions without the need for intermediaries. In this section, we will explore the concept of smart contracts, their benefits, and their implications for digital asset custody. Understanding smart contracts is crucial for custodians and asset owners to leverage the full potential of this innovative technology.

At its core, a smart contract is a self-executing agreement that automatically enforces the terms and conditions encoded within its code. Smart contracts operate on blockchain platforms, typically leveraging the solidity programming language for Ethereum-based contracts. These contracts facilitate the secure and reliable execution of transactions, reducing the need for intermediaries and providing a new level of trust and efficiency in value exchange.

Smart contract execution process

One of the key benefits of smart contracts is their ability to automate and streamline transactions. Traditional financial agreements often involve multiple intermediaries, complex paperwork, and manual processes, leading to delays, human errors, and increased costs. Smart contracts eliminate these inefficiencies by automating the execution of predefined conditions and removing the need for intermediaries. This automation streamlines the transaction process, reduces costs, and accelerates settlement times.

The transparency and immutability of blockchain technology enhance the trustworthiness of smart contracts. Once a smart contract is deployed on a blockchain, its code becomes immutable, meaning it cannot be modified or tampered with. This immutability ensures that the agreed-upon terms and conditions cannot be altered, providing a high level of trust and eliminating the risk of manipulation or disputes. Asset owners and custodians can confidently engage in transactions knowing that the smart contract will enforce the agreed-upon rules without bias or interference.

Smart contracts also enable the programmability of digital assets, allowing for the creation of sophisticated financial instruments and complex workflows. Through the use of conditional statements, loops, and external data inputs, smart contracts can execute complex logic and implement intricate business rules. This programmability opens up new possibilities for digital asset custody, including the automation of custody processes, the creation of escrow services, and the integration with decentralized finance (DeFi) protocols.

In the context of digital asset custody, smart contracts offer several advantages for custodians and asset owners. First and foremost, smart contracts provide enhanced security. The automation and cryptographic security measures inherent in smart contracts significantly reduce the risk of human error and manipulation. The terms of custody agreements can be encoded into smart contracts, ensuring that custody operations are executed precisely as agreed upon. This reduces the potential for unauthorized access, fraud, or disputes, enhancing the security and integrity of custodial services.

Smart contracts also improve operational efficiency for custodians. By automating various custody-related processes, such as asset transfers, account reconciliations, and compliance checks, custodians can streamline their operations and reduce manual interventions. This automation reduces the likelihood of errors, enhances data accuracy, and increases the speed of transaction processing. Custodians can focus on value-added services and client interactions, knowing that the custody processes are executed accurately and efficiently through smart contracts.

Smart contract schema

The integration of smart contracts with decentralized finance (DeFi) protocols presents new opportunities and challenges for custodians. DeFi platforms leverage smart contracts to offer open, permissionless financial services without intermediaries. Custodians can explore partnerships and integrations with DeFi protocols to enable secure custody of decentralized assets and facilitate value exchange within these ecosystems. However, custodians must also navigate the unique risks associated with DeFi, such as smart contract vulnerabilities and the complexity of custody solutions for decentralized assets.

Despite the many benefits of smart contracts, there are also challenges and considerations for custodians. Smart contract vulnerabilities, such as coding errors or security flaws, can lead to financial losses or exploitation. Custodians must conduct thorough code audits, implement best practices for secure smart contract development, and stay informed about emerging security techniques to mitigate these risks. Additionally, custodians must ensure compatibility and interoperability with different blockchain platforms and smart contract standards to effectively custody a wide range of digital assets.

Legal and regulatory considerations also come into play when dealing with smart contracts. As smart contracts automate the execution of transactions and agreements, legal frameworks may need to adapt to accommodate these technological innovations. Custodians must navigate the legal implications of smart contracts, including contract enforceability, legal jurisdiction, and dispute resolution mechanisms. Engaging legal experts and collaborating with regulators can help custodians align their operations with existing legal frameworks and contribute to the development of regulatory clarity in the digital asset custody space.

In conclusion, smart contracts have transformed the landscape of digital asset custody by automating value exchange and enhancing security and efficiency. The ability to encode and enforce contract terms in code eliminates the need for intermediaries, streamlines transactions, and provides a new level of trust and transparency. Custodians can leverage smart contracts to enhance security, improve operational efficiency, and explore opportunities in the evolving DeFi ecosystem. By understanding the benefits and challenges associated with smart contracts, custodians can harness the full potential of this technology and provide innovative and reliable custody services in the digital asset space.

1.10 The Impact of Digital Assets on Traditional Finance

The emergence of digital assets has brought about significant disruptions and transformative potential for the traditional finance industry. As digital assets gain prominence and adoption, their impact on traditional finance becomes increasingly evident. In this section, we will explore the implications of digital assets on various aspects of traditional finance, highlighting the key areas of impact and the opportunities and challenges they present.

1.10.1 Disintermediation and Peer-to-Peer Transactions

One of the most profound impacts of digital assets on traditional finance is the potential for disintermediation. Digital assets, operating on decentralized networks such as blockchain, enable direct peer-to-peer transactions without the need for intermediaries such as banks or financial institutions. This disintermediation has the potential to reshape various financial activities, including payments, remittances, lending, and fundraising.

By removing intermediaries, digital assets can streamline transactions, reduce costs, and enhance efficiency. For example, cross-border payments and remittances can become faster, cheaper, and more accessible by leveraging digital assets. Peer-to-peer lending platforms can connect borrowers and lenders directly, eliminating the need for traditional financial intermediaries. Additionally, digital assets enable decentralized fundraising mechanisms, such as initial coin offerings (ICOs) or security token offerings (STOs), which provide alternative avenues for capital formation.

However, disintermediation also introduces challenges and regulatory considerations. As traditional financial institutions face potential disruptions to their business models, they must adapt to the changing landscape and explore opportunities to integrate digital assets into their operations. Regulators must establish frameworks to ensure consumer protection, market integrity, and financial stability in the context of digital assets. Custodians play a crucial role in bridging the gap between the decentralized nature of digital assets and the need for regulatory compliance and consumer protection.

1.10.2 Financial Inclusion and Access to Capital

Digital assets have the potential to improve financial inclusion by providing access to financial services for individuals and businesses that are underserved or excluded from the traditional financial system. Digital wallets and mobile applications allow users to securely store, send, and receive digital assets, eliminating the need for traditional bank accounts. This opens up opportunities for individuals in underbanked regions or without access to traditional financial institutions to participate in the global financial ecosystem.

Moreover, digital assets enable fractional ownership and micro-investing, allowing individuals to invest in assets that were previously inaccessible due to high entry barriers. Tokenization of real-world assets, such as real estate or artwork, enables fractional ownership and liquidity, expanding investment opportunities for a broader range of investors. This democratization of investment can stimulate economic growth and provide individuals with new avenues to build wealth.

1.10.3 Automation, Efficiency, and Cost Reduction

Digital assets and the underlying technologies, such as blockchain and smart contracts, offer automation, efficiency, and cost reduction opportunities in various financial processes. Through the automation of transactions, settlements, and recordkeeping, digital assets can streamline processes, reduce human errors, and eliminate manual reconciliation. This increased automation can lead to significant cost savings for financial institutions.

For example, in the realm of securities settlement, traditional processes involve multiple intermediaries, complex paperwork, and lengthy settlement periods. By leveraging digital assets and smart contracts, securities settlement can become faster, more transparent, and less prone to errors. This can result in reduced settlement times, lower operational costs, and improved liquidity for market participants.

Furthermore, the transparency and traceability of digital assets can enhance risk management and compliance processes. Transaction data recorded on the blockchain provides an immutable audit trail, simplifying regulatory reporting, and facilitating compliance monitoring. This transparency can contribute to reducing fraud, money laundering, and other financial crimes, leading to a more secure and trusted financial system.

However, the adoption of digital assets and the underlying technologies requires significant investment in infrastructure, talent, and regulatory frameworks. Financial institutions need to assess the costs and benefits of implementing digital asset solutions and strike a balance between innovation and risk management. Collaboration with technology providers, fintech startups, and regulatory authorities can foster the development of scalable and secure digital asset solutions.

1.10.4 Regulatory Challenges and Compliance

The rise of digital assets poses regulatory challenges for traditional finance. Regulators worldwide are grappling with the task of developing appropriate frameworks to govern digital assets while protecting investors, ensuring market integrity, and mitigating potential systemic risks. Regulatory considerations include investor protection, consumer rights, anti-money laundering (AML) and know-your-customer (KYC) requirements, taxation, securities regulations, and data protection.

Custodians operating in the digital asset space must navigate these evolving regulatory landscapes and develop robust compliance programs to ensure adherence to applicable laws and regulations. This includes implementing AML and KYC procedures, establishing robust cybersecurity measures, and maintaining compliance with tax obligations. Custodians play a critical role in building trust and confidence in the digital asset ecosystem by providing secure and compliant custodial services.

Collaboration between custodians, regulators, and industry participants is vital to strike the right balance between innovation and regulation. Regulators must foster an enabling environment that encourages responsible innovation while protecting market participants. Industry associations and working groups can play a pivotal role in advocating for sensible regulatory frameworks, sharing best practices, and fostering open dialogue between stakeholders.

In conclusion, digital assets have a profound impact on traditional finance, bringing disintermediation, financial inclusion, automation, and regulatory challenges. The potential for peer-to-peer transactions, improved access to capital, automation of financial processes, and cost reduction presents opportunities for innovation and efficiency. However, custodians and financial institutions must navigate regulatory considerations, adapt to changing business models, and strike a balance between embracing digital assets and ensuring compliance, security, and market integrity.

1.11 Tokenization use cases

Structured products, comprising a diverse range of financial assets and derivatives, have long been a popular choice for investors seeking specific returns. However, the issuance processes for these products have often lagged behind in terms of efficiency and innovation. Enter the era of tokenization and digitization.

There are challenges associated with traditional issuance processes and explore the significant benefits that tokenization brings to structured product creation and issuance.

Challenges in the Current Issuance Processes

In the United States, structured product issuance heavily relies on physical documents and traditional bookkeeping systems. These products are subsequently traded on exchanges, with clearing and financial transactions managed through established systems like DTCC. This labor-intensive process involves multiple complex steps, leading to various challenges:

- Manual and Sequential Processes: The current procedures heavily rely on manual and paper-based methods, which follow a strict sequential order. This often leads to delays and increased costs, as steps cannot be completed asynchronously or effectively monitored.
- Lengthy Clearing and Settlement Cycles: Clearing and settlement processes are time-consuming, with extended timelines ranging from T+3 in public markets to as long as 10 business days for private securities. These prolonged cycles result in financial costs and asset lock-up.
- Data Reconciliation Complexities: Despite continuous reconciliations, multiple versions of the truth persist. These reconciliations contribute to higher issuance costs.
- Settlement Risk: Settlement risk arises from upfront purchases and delayed account credits, introducing a level of uncertainty. Counterparty risk also exists until successful settlement is achieved.
- Lack of Transparency: Limited transparency within the asset creation and issuance processes is due to various systems and a highly manual approach. The absence of an electronic audit trail makes tracing and observability extremely challenging.

- Multiple Intermediaries: The involvement of multiple intermediaries adds complexity to the processes, requiring coordination among various parties. This separation between asset definition and workflow rules further complicates the process.

The Transformative Power of Distributed Ledger Technology (DLT)

Distributed Ledger Technology (DLT), specifically blockchain, holds immense potential in revolutionizing structured product issuance by replacing physical documents with fully digitized "smart" securities. These smart contracts, executed on a blockchain-based platform, offer greater efficiency by reducing reliance on intermediaries. Here are some key benefits:

- Streamlined Digital Workflow: DLT introduces a digital paradigm where documents seamlessly integrate into the digital asset's definition. Multi-party workflows become concurrent and asynchronous, significantly reducing administrative overhead and costs.
- Swift and Secure Settlement: Smart contracts automate the execution of terms and conditions, resulting in faster and more cost-effective transaction processes. Real-time settlement reduces capital costs, systemic risk, and post-trade process complexities.
- Unified Data Source: DLT establishes a single, unalterable source of truth through a unified master book. This simplifies data management by eliminating the need for additional services and providers.
- Risk Mitigation and Automation: DLT supports atomic settlement, enabling real-time Delivery versus Payment (DVP) and Payment versus Payment (PVP). Full lifecycle automation reduces complexity and potential errors.
- Enhanced Transparency: Clear roles, responsibilities, and immutable records enhance transparency in the issuance lifecycle. A unified master book provides real-time visibility into asset positions.
- Streamlined Intermediation: Direct issuance of digital securities on a distributed ledger accelerates matching of buyers and sellers, reduces intermediary fees, and automates processes like dividends and voting.

Debt Tokenization: Revolutionizing the Financial Industry

Debt tokenization, the process of converting traditional debt instruments such as loans and bonds into digital tokens on blockchain or distributed ledgers, has gained significant traction throughout the financial services industry. In 2023, major financial institutions such as Goldman Sachs, UBS, and HSBC actively engaged in digital bond issuances.

The benefits of tokenizing debt include:
- Paperless Creation: By eliminating physical certificates and manual mark-ups, the risk of errors is reduced, and valuable time is saved.
- Streamlined Interactions: A common Distributed Ledger Technology (DLT) platform enables efficient collaboration between different parties involved in debt issuance, settlement, payment, and redemption processes.
- Seamless Settlement: Debt transfer and cash payment can be conducted on a common DLT platform, reducing settlement delays and risks.
- End-to-End DLT Adoption: From primary issuance to secondary trading, coupon payment, and maturity redemption, DLT streamlines processes, reduces costs, and improves operational efficiency.
- Enhanced Transparency: DLT enables real-time data synchronization, promoting transparency and consistency among platform participants.

Equity Tokenization: Unlocking New Possibilities in Capital Raising

The traditional method of equity capital raising presents limitations for issuers, such as a small network of private equity investors and a lack of secondary market solutions. In response, equity tokenization offers a practical solution by digitizing shares using distributed ledger technology, like blockchain.

Equity tokenization brings several benefits:
- Digital and Programmable Equity: By creating digital tokens that represent share ownership, equity transfers become instantaneous, and smart contracts can automate processes like dividend payments, leading to time and cost savings.
- Instant Booking and Settlement: Ledger-based securities can be directly booked with banks, reducing settlement times and associated costs by eliminating intermediaries.
- Broader Investor Base: Equity tokenization makes private equity accessible to a wider range of investors, reducing barriers to entry outside of institutional investment realms.
- Secondary Markets: Issuers can provide liquidity to shareholders and employees through electronic trading, introducing new price discovery mechanisms and enhancing transparency.
- To tokenize equity, a proven process can be followed:
- Legal Preparation: Adapt the corporation's articles of association to include ledger-based securities and obtain board approval for tokenization rules and registration.
- Smart Contract Setup: Identify audited smart contracts that align with regulatory requirements for ledger-based securities.
- Investor Material Preparation: Prepare materials for investors if raising funds, following technology-neutral regulations.
- Board Consensus and Regulations: Record a resolution to tokenize shares in line with the articles of association and tokenization regulations.
- Trading Admission Preparation: Open an account within a regulated trading platform, like Taurus, to participate in trading.

Equity tokenization revolutionizes capital raising practices, offering efficiency, accessibility, and transparency in the issuance, transfer, and trading of equity. With a well-defined regulatory framework and technological advancements, this innovative approach is transforming the landscape of private company financing.

2. The Importance of Custodians in Digital Asset Management

2.1 The Role of Custodians in Safeguarding Digital Assets

In the rapidly evolving landscape of digital assets, custodians play a critical role in safeguarding these valuable assets. As the adoption of cryptocurrencies, digital securities, and other tokenized assets continues to grow, the need for trusted custodial services becomes paramount. In this section, we will explore the essential role of custodians in securing and managing digital assets, emphasizing the importance of trust, security, and reliability.

Custodians act as trusted intermediaries responsible for the safekeeping and management of digital assets on behalf of individuals and institutions. With the rise of blockchain technology, which enables peer-to-peer transactions and eliminates the need for intermediaries, the role of custodians has become even more significant. They serve as the guardians of private keys, the digital credentials that grant access to digital assets, and ensure the secure custody and availability of these assets.

One of the primary functions of custodians is to provide secure storage for private keys. Private keys are critical components that enable asset owners to authenticate and authorize transactions. Custodians employ various security measures to protect private keys from theft, loss, or unauthorized access. These measures include robust encryption, physical security protocols, multi-factor authentication, and secure data storage.

By entrusting their assets to custodians, asset owners benefit from enhanced security and protection against cyber threats. Custodians employ sophisticated cybersecurity measures to mitigate the risk of unauthorized access or hacking attempts. They invest in cutting-edge technologies and engage security experts to ensure the confidentiality, integrity, and availability of digital assets under their custody.

Moreover, custodians play a vital role in providing operational resilience. They establish redundant systems and backup protocols to ensure the continuous availability of custodial services. In the event of system failures, natural disasters, or cyber incidents, custodians have robust disaster recovery plans in place to minimize disruptions and protect the assets they hold. Operational resilience is crucial to maintain trust and confidence in custodial services, especially in times of crisis or unforeseen events.

Trust is the cornerstone of custodial services. Custodians must build and maintain trust by demonstrating their integrity, reliability, and adherence to industry best practices. Transparency is a key element in establishing trust.

Custodians should provide clear and comprehensive information about their security measures, operational processes, compliance practices, and audit procedures. Open communication channels and responsive customer support further contribute to building trust with asset owners.

Custodians also play a vital role in regulatory compliance. As the digital asset ecosystem becomes more regulated, custodians must adhere to relevant laws, regulations, and industry standards. Compliance with anti-money laundering (AML), know-your-customer (KYC), and other financial crime prevention measures is essential. Custodians must implement robust AML and KYC procedures to ensure the legitimacy of transactions and protect against illicit activities.

In addition to security and compliance, custodians provide asset owners with peace of mind. Digital assets are often associated with high-value investments, financial transactions, and personal wealth. The knowledge that their assets are in the hands of trusted custodians who prioritize security and reliability allows asset owners to focus on their core activities without the constant worry of asset protection.

Furthermore, custodians can offer value-added services to enhance the overall management of digital assets. These services may include reporting and analytics, portfolio management tools, tax reporting assistance, and integration with financial platforms. By providing comprehensive solutions, custodians enable asset owners to have a holistic view of their digital asset portfolios and facilitate seamless asset management.

As the digital asset landscape continues to evolve, custodians must adapt and evolve with it. They need to stay abreast of emerging technologies, regulatory developments, and industry best practices. Custodians should actively engage in research and development to continuously improve their security measures, operational processes, and service offerings. Collaboration with industry stakeholders, participation in standardization efforts, and knowledge sharing are critical to foster innovation and drive the evolution of custodial services.

In conclusion, custodians play a vital role in safeguarding digital assets and ensuring the trust, security, and reliability of custody services. By providing secure storage, robust cybersecurity measures, operational resilience, and regulatory compliance, custodians instill confidence in asset owners and contribute to the broader adoption and utilization of digital assets. As the digital asset ecosystem continues to grow and mature, custodians must remain proactive, adaptable, and committed to delivering exceptional custodial services in an ever-changing landscape.

2.2 Trust and Security: Building Confidence in Digital Asset Custody

Trust and security are paramount in the realm of digital asset custody. As individuals and institutions increasingly embrace digital assets, the role of custodians in providing a secure and trustworthy environment becomes critical. In this section, we will explore the importance of trust and security in digital asset custody, emphasizing the measures custodians employ to build confidence among asset owners.

Trust forms the foundation of any custodial relationship. Asset owners must have confidence that their digital assets are in safe hands, protected from theft, loss, or unauthorized access. Custodians must establish and maintain trust through transparent practices, robust security measures, and a track record of reliability.

Transparency is a key element in building trust. Custodians should provide clear and comprehensive information about their security practices, operational procedures, and compliance measures. Asset owners need to understand how their assets are stored, how access is controlled, and what measures are in place to protect against cyber threats. By being transparent about their custodial processes, custodians demonstrate their commitment to accountability and instill confidence in asset owners.

Robust security measures are fundamental to ensuring the safety of digital assets. Custodians employ a range of security protocols to protect against cyber threats, unauthorized access, and theft. These measures may include multi-factor authentication, encryption, physical security controls, and secure data storage. Custodians regularly assess and update their security infrastructure to address emerging threats and vulnerabilities. By implementing best-in-class security practices, custodians offer asset owners peace of mind and mitigate the risk of asset compromise.

Furthermore, custodians should engage with independent auditors and undergo regular security audits. External audits provide an objective evaluation of custodial practices, offering an additional layer of assurance for asset owners. Audits can assess the effectiveness of security measures, identify potential vulnerabilities, and validate compliance with industry standards. Sharing audit reports with asset owners demonstrates a commitment to transparency and accountability, further strengthening trust in custodial services.

AML and industry standards is crucial in building trust in digital asset custody. Custodians must adhere to relevant laws, regulations, and best practices, including anti-money laundering (AML), know-your-customer (KYC), and other financial crime prevention measures. Compliance programs should be robust, comprehensive, and regularly reviewed to ensure ongoing adherence to regulatory obligations. Custodians that demonstrate a strong commitment to compliance inspire confidence and demonstrate their dedication to operating within legal boundaries.

Partnerships and collaborations can also contribute to building trust in digital asset custody. Custodians can forge relationships with reputable industry players, such as financial institutions, blockchain technology providers, and cybersecurity firms. These partnerships allow custodians to leverage the expertise and resources of established entities, enhancing the security and reliability of their custodial services. By aligning themselves with trusted partners, custodians gain credibility and instill confidence in asset owners.

Customer support and responsiveness are crucial components of building trust. Custodians should provide timely and effective customer support to address inquiries, resolve issues, and provide reassurance to asset owners. Responsive customer service demonstrates a commitment to client satisfaction and reinforces the custodian's dedication to building strong, long-term relationships. Clear communication channels and proactive engagement contribute to fostering trust and confidence in the custodial relationship.

Additionally, custodians can leverage the power of technology to enhance trust and security. For example, they can utilize blockchain technology to increase transparency and immutability in custody processes. By leveraging distributed ledger technology, custodians can provide asset owners with real-time visibility into their asset holdings and transactions, ensuring transparency and accountability. Implementing advanced technological solutions demonstrates a commitment to innovation and reinforces the custodian's dedication to maintaining a secure and efficient custody environment.

Education and awareness initiatives also play a vital role in building trust. Custodians should provide educational resources, training materials, and guidelines to asset owners, helping them understand the risks and security best practices associated with digital asset custody. By empowering asset owners with knowledge, custodians enable them to make informed decisions and actively participate in securing their digital assets. Education initiatives demonstrate custodians' commitment to the well-being of asset owners and foster a sense of shared responsibility.

In conclusion, trust and security are essential components of digital asset custody. Custodians must prioritize transparency, robust security measures, regulatory compliance, and responsive customer support to build confidence among asset owners. By demonstrating their commitment to protecting assets, custodians foster trust, enabling the broader adoption and utilization of digital assets. As the digital asset ecosystem continues to evolve, custodians must remain vigilant, adaptable, and committed to providing secure and reliable custody services.

2.3 Compliance and Regulatory Considerations for Custodians

In the world of digital asset custody, compliance with regulations and adherence to industry standards are paramount. As the digital asset ecosystem continues to evolve, custodians must navigate a complex landscape of regulatory requirements to ensure the security, transparency, and legal compliance of their custodial services. In this section, we will explore the compliance and regulatory considerations that custodians face, emphasizing the importance of robust compliance programs, regulatory frameworks, and industry standards.

The digital asset space is subject to a rapidly evolving regulatory environment. Governments and regulatory authorities worldwide are grappling with the challenges posed by digital assets, aiming to strike a balance between fostering innovation and protecting investors and the financial system. Custodians, as key players in the custody of digital assets, must stay abreast of regulatory developments, understand their obligations, and implement robust compliance programs.

Anti-money laundering (AML) and know-your-customer (KYC) regulations form a crucial aspect of custodial compliance. Custodians must implement stringent AML and KYC procedures to prevent the use of digital assets for illicit purposes, such as money laundering, terrorist financing, or other financial crimes. These procedures involve verifying the identity of customers, conducting due diligence on transactions, monitoring for suspicious activities, and reporting any suspicious or unusual transactions to the relevant authorities.

Additionally, custodians must consider the evolving regulatory landscape surrounding digital securities and other tokenized assets. Depending on the jurisdiction, these assets may be subject to securities regulations, which require custodians to comply with specific requirements related to custody, reporting, and investor protection. Custodians must ensure they are operating within the legal boundaries and meeting the regulatory obligations associated with these assets.

The complexity of cross-border transactions adds an additional layer of compliance considerations for custodians. International transactions involve navigating different regulatory frameworks, AML requirements, and sanctions regimes. Custodians must have robust processes in place to address cross-border compliance challenges, ensuring compliance with both local and international regulations. This includes understanding and adhering to sanctions lists, conducting appropriate due diligence on international counterparties, and maintaining compliance with cross-border reporting requirements.

Custodians must also consider data protection and privacy regulations. The custody of digital assets involves the collection, storage, and processing of personal and transactional data. Custodians must implement appropriate data protection measures, including data encryption, access controls, and data retention policies, to ensure compliance with applicable privacy regulations. They should also inform asset owners about how their data is collected, used, and protected, fostering transparency and trust.

Regulatory compliance is not a one-time endeavor but an ongoing commitment. Custodians must maintain vigilant compliance programs that adapt to regulatory changes and evolving best practices. This involves conducting regular risk assessments, staying updated on regulatory developments, and engaging in industry discussions and collaborations. By actively participating in regulatory dialogues, custodians can contribute to the shaping of regulatory frameworks and ensure that they remain relevant and effective.

Engaging with regulatory authorities and building strong relationships is another critical aspect of compliance. Custodians should proactively communicate with regulators, seeking clarification on regulatory requirements, and providing feedback on the practical implications of proposed regulations. By collaborating with regulators, custodians can contribute to the development of practical and effective regulatory frameworks that address the unique challenges of digital asset custody.

Adherence to industry standards and best practices is also vital for custodians. Participating in industry consortia, standardization bodies, and self-regulatory organizations can help custodians establish best practices, share insights, and benchmark their operations against industry standards. Compliance with recognized industry standards demonstrates a commitment to professionalism, accountability, and adherence to industry norms.

Moreover, custodians must establish robust internal controls and governance structures to ensure compliance with regulatory obligations. This includes assigning clear roles and responsibilities, implementing policies and procedures, and conducting regular audits and internal reviews. Internal controls help ensure that custodians operate within the bounds of applicable regulations, maintain accurate records, and safeguard assets from unauthorized access or misuse.

Lastly, custodians must embrace technological advancements to facilitate compliance efforts. Regulatory technology (RegTech) solutions can streamline compliance processes, automate reporting, and enhance the effectiveness of compliance programs. By leveraging advanced data analytics, artificial intelligence, and blockchain technology, custodians can enhance their compliance capabilities, identify potential risks, and demonstrate adherence to regulatory obligations.

In conclusion, compliance with regulatory requirements is of utmost importance for custodians in the digital asset space. AML, KYC, data protection, cross-border transactions, and evolving regulatory frameworks pose significant challenges that custodians must address. By implementing robust compliance programs, actively engaging with regulators, adhering to industry standards, and leveraging technology, custodians can ensure the security, transparency, and legal compliance of their custodial services. Compliance is not just a legal obligation but a fundamental aspect of building trust and confidence in digital asset custody.

2.4 Operational Resilience: Ensuring Reliable Custodial Services

Operational resilience is a critical aspect of digital asset custody, ensuring the reliable and uninterrupted provision of custodial services. As custodians safeguard and manage digital assets on behalf of individuals and institutions, they must establish robust operational processes, implement redundancy measures, and mitigate operational risks. In this section, we will explore the importance of operational resilience in digital asset custody, highlighting the measures custodians employ to ensure the continuity and reliability of their services.

The custodial industry operates in a dynamic and technologically advanced environment, where disruptions can have significant consequences. Operational resilience encompasses the ability of custodians to anticipate, prevent, respond to, and recover from operational disruptions, such as system failures, cyber incidents, natural disasters, or human errors. It involves the implementation of comprehensive strategies, policies, and protocols to minimize the impact of disruptions and ensure the seamless functioning of custodial services.

One key aspect of operational resilience is the establishment of robust disaster recovery plans. Custodians must have well-defined procedures in place to recover operations swiftly and efficiently in the event of a disruption. These plans include backup systems, redundant infrastructure, and failover mechanisms to ensure that custodial services can continue without significant interruption. Regular testing and evaluation of disaster recovery plans help identify weaknesses and enhance the effectiveness of these measures.

Custodians must also consider the physical security of their facilities and assets. Adequate physical security measures, such as access controls, surveillance systems, and secure storage facilities, are crucial to safeguarding the physical infrastructure that supports custodial operations. By implementing strict physical security protocols, custodians can mitigate the risk of unauthorized access, theft, or damage to critical assets and infrastructure.

Furthermore, custodians must invest in robust cybersecurity measures to protect against cyber threats. Cybersecurity is a significant concern in the digital asset space, given the potential financial and reputational damage that can result from security breaches. Custodians employ various cybersecurity measures, including network security, encryption, intrusion detection systems, and regular vulnerability assessments. They continuously monitor and update their security measures to stay ahead of emerging threats and vulnerabilities.

To enhance operational resilience, custodians should establish comprehensive incident response plans. These plans outline the procedures to be followed in the event of an operational disruption, ensuring that appropriate actions are taken promptly and effectively. Incident response plans typically involve clear lines of communication, escalation protocols, and the involvement of key stakeholders to coordinate response efforts. By having a well-defined incident response framework, custodians can minimize the impact of disruptions and mitigate potential risks.

Custodians must also address the risk of human errors, which can have significant consequences in the custody of digital assets. Training and education programs play a crucial role in mitigating this risk. Custodians should provide comprehensive training to their staff, emphasizing the importance of adhering to operational procedures, following security protocols, and maintaining vigilance in their day-to-day activities. Ongoing education ensures that custodial staff are equipped with the necessary knowledge and skills to effectively navigate operational risks.

The use of automation and technology can significantly enhance operational resilience. Custodians can leverage advanced technologies, such as robotic process automation (RPA) and artificial intelligence (AI), to streamline operational processes, reduce manual errors, and enhance efficiency. Automation can also provide real-time monitoring and alerting capabilities, allowing custodians to proactively identify and address potential issues before they escalate.

Regular audits and independent reviews are essential components of operational resilience. Custodians should engage external auditors to assess their operational processes, controls, and risk management frameworks. These audits provide an objective evaluation of custodial practices, identifying areas for improvement and validating the effectiveness of operational resilience measures. Sharing audit reports with stakeholders demonstrates a commitment to transparency and accountability, further strengthening trust in custodial services.

Custodians must establish strong governance structures to ensure effective operational resilience. This includes clearly defined roles and responsibilities, accountability mechanisms, and internal control frameworks. Regular monitoring and reporting on operational resilience indicators help identify potential risks, assess the effectiveness of operational processes, and drive continuous improvement. By establishing a culture of operational excellence and accountability, custodians can enhance their ability to deliver reliable and secure custodial services.

In conclusion, operational resilience is a critical component of digital asset custody, ensuring the reliability, continuity, and security of custodial services. By establishing robust disaster recovery plans, implementing physical and cybersecurity measures, developing incident response frameworks, addressing human error risks, leveraging automation and technology, and conducting regular audits, custodians can mitigate operational risks and enhance their ability to withstand disruptions. Operational resilience is essential to instill confidence in asset owners and maintain the trust required for the effective custody of digital assets.

2.5 The Evolution of Custodial Technologies and Infrastructure

In the ever-evolving landscape of digital asset custody, custodians must continually adapt and leverage technological advancements to meet the growing demands of the industry. The emergence of blockchain technology, decentralized finance (DeFi), and other innovative solutions has transformed the custodial landscape, offering new opportunities and challenges. In this section, we will explore the evolution of custodial technologies and infrastructure, highlighting the key developments and their impact on digital asset custody.

Blockchain technology has played a significant role in reshaping the custodial space. The inherent properties of blockchain, including immutability, transparency, and decentralization, offer unique benefits for custodial operations. Custodians have embraced blockchain to enhance the security, efficiency, and trustworthiness of their services. By leveraging blockchain technology, custodians can provide transparent and auditable custody solutions, allowing asset owners to verify the integrity and ownership of their digital assets.

The introduction of smart contracts has further revolutionized the custodial landscape. Smart contracts are self-executing agreements that automatically enforce the terms and conditions encoded within them. Custodians can utilize smart contracts to facilitate secure custody and automate various custody-related processes, such as asset transfers, escrow services, and compliance checks. Smart contracts provide efficiency, transparency, and programmability, enhancing the overall custodial experience for asset owners.

Decentralized finance (DeFi) has emerged as a disruptive force in the digital asset ecosystem, presenting both opportunities and challenges for custodians. DeFi platforms leverage blockchain technology to provide open, permissionless financial services without intermediaries. While DeFi enables greater financial inclusivity and autonomy, it also introduces complexities for custodians. Custodians must navigate the decentralized nature of DeFi, exploring how to effectively custody decentralized assets while ensuring the security and compliance of custodial services.

Multi-signature schemes have gained prominence as an additional layer of security in digital asset custody. Multi-signature, or multi-sig, requires multiple authorized signatures to execute a transaction. This feature mitigates the risk of a single point of failure, as multiple parties must collectively authorize asset transfers. Custodians can leverage multi-signature schemes to enhance the security and integrity of custodial operations, ensuring that no single entity has complete control over the assets.

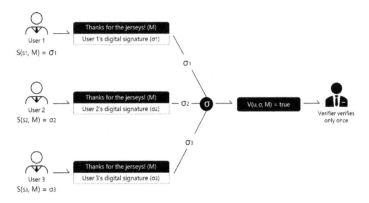

Multisignature scheme

Hardware security modules (HSMs) are specialized devices that provide secure key management and cryptographic operations. Custodians employ HSMs to store and protect private keys, ensuring the integrity and confidentiality of digital assets. HSMs offer tamper-resistant hardware, strong encryption capabilities, and access controls, making them a crucial component of custodial infrastructure. By utilizing HSMs, custodians enhance the security posture of their custody services and protect against unauthorized access or key compromise.

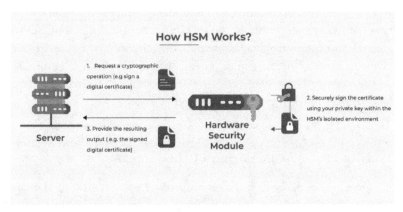

HSM scheme

Privacy-preserving technologies are becoming increasingly relevant in the custodial space. As digital assets gain mainstream adoption, privacy considerations come to the forefront. Custodians must balance the transparency requirements of custody services with the need to protect asset owner privacy. Privacy-enhancing technologies, such as zero-knowledge proofs, secure multi-party computation, and confidential transactions, allow custodians to provide secure and privacy-preserving custody solutions, ensuring the confidentiality of sensitive information while maintaining the transparency necessary for auditability.

The integration of digital assets with traditional financial infrastructure is a significant development in custodial technologies. As digital assets bridge the gap between traditional and digital finance, custodians must ensure interoperability and seamless connectivity between these systems. Custodians can leverage application programming interfaces (APIs) and standardized protocols to facilitate the integration of digital assets with existing financial infrastructure, allowing for efficient asset transfers and enhanced liquidity.

Cloud computing has transformed the scalability and flexibility of custodial infrastructure. Cloud-based custody solutions offer on-demand access to computational resources, storage capacity, and infrastructure management. Custodians can leverage cloud computing to scale their operations, reduce costs, and ensure business continuity. However, custodians must also carefully consider the security and compliance implications of cloud-based solutions, implementing robust security measures and adhering to relevant data protection regulations.

The emergence of custodial service providers tailored specifically for institutional clients has reshaped the custodial landscape. Institutional custodians offer sophisticated custody solutions that cater to the unique needs of institutional investors, such as compliance with fiduciary obligations, reporting requirements, and risk management frameworks. These custodians provide advanced security measures, asset segregation, and comprehensive reporting capabilities, allowing institutions to confidently engage with digital assets while meeting their regulatory and risk management obligations.

The evolution of custodial technologies and infrastructure has also given rise to interoperability challenges. As the digital asset ecosystem expands, custodians must navigate the interoperability of different blockchain networks and asset protocols. Standards and protocols such as InterBlockchain Communication (IBC) and cross-chain bridges facilitate interoperability, enabling custodians to custody and manage assets across multiple blockchains. Custodians must stay informed about interoperability solutions and actively engage in industry discussions to ensure seamless asset transfers and custody across various networks.

In conclusion, the evolution of custodial technologies and infrastructure has significantly impacted the digital asset custody landscape. Blockchain technology, smart contracts, multi-signature schemes, HSMs, privacy-preserving technologies, and integration with traditional financial infrastructure have transformed the way custodians secure, manage, and transfer digital assets. Custodians must embrace these technological advancements, adapt to the rise of DeFi, and navigate interoperability challenges to provide secure, reliable, and innovative custodial services in the dynamic digital asset ecosystem.

2.6 Custodial Best Practices: Safeguarding Against Cyber Threats

Custodial best practices are essential in the digital asset industry to protect assets and maintain the trust of asset owners. As the custody of digital assets involves managing sensitive data and controlling access to valuable assets, custodians must prioritize robust cybersecurity measures to safeguard against cyber threats. In this section, we will explore the key custodial best practices that custodians should implement to mitigate cyber risks and protect digital assets.

2.6.1 Comprehensive Security Framework

Custodians should establish a comprehensive security framework that encompasses various layers of protection to defend against cyber threats. This framework should include physical security measures, network security, system monitoring, access controls, and incident response protocols.

Physical security measures involve securing physical access to data centers or server rooms where digital assets are stored. This includes restricted access, surveillance systems, and measures to prevent unauthorized entry or physical theft.

Network security is crucial to protect digital assets from unauthorized access or attacks. Custodians should implement robust firewalls, intrusion detection systems, and regular vulnerability assessments to identify and address potential vulnerabilities in their networks. Secure network architecture, including segregated environments and network segmentation, helps to limit the impact of a potential breach.

System monitoring plays a vital role in detecting and responding to security incidents. Custodians should implement real-time monitoring systems that track network traffic, system logs, and user activities to identify suspicious behavior or potential security breaches. Security information and event management (SIEM) tools can help centralize and analyze security logs and alerts for proactive threat detection.

Access controls are critical in protecting digital assets from unauthorized access. Custodians should implement strong authentication mechanisms, such as multi-factor authentication, to ensure that only authorized individuals can access sensitive systems or perform critical operations. Role-based access controls should be established to assign appropriate permissions and restrict access to specific functions or data based on job responsibilities.

Incident response protocols are essential for effectively managing security incidents. Custodians should establish incident response plans that outline procedures for identifying, containing, and mitigating security incidents. Regular testing and drills can help ensure the effectiveness of these response plans and enable custodians to respond swiftly and effectively in case of a cyber attack.

2.6.2 Secure Storage and Key Management

The secure storage of digital assets and the proper management of cryptographic keys are paramount for custodians. Custodians should implement secure storage solutions, such as hardware security modules (HSMs) or cold storage options, to safeguard private keys and digital asset backups.

Hardware security modules provide tamper-resistant storage and cryptographic operations, protecting private keys from unauthorized access or extraction. Cold storage options, such as offline wallets or air-gapped systems, ensure that private keys are stored offline and inaccessible to online threats.

Custodians should also establish robust key management practices. This includes secure key generation, key rotation, and key backup procedures. Key encryption and secure key sharing mechanisms should be implemented to protect keys during transmission or storage.

Furthermore, custodians should carefully consider the distribution of cryptographic keys to prevent single points of failure. Multi-signature schemes, where multiple authorized signatures are required to execute transactions, can enhance security by preventing a single compromised key from authorizing unauthorized transactions.

2.6.3 Ongoing Security Education and Training

Custodians must prioritize ongoing security education and training programs for their employees. Cybersecurity threats are continuously evolving, and custodians must ensure that their staff is equipped with the knowledge and skills necessary to identify and respond to emerging threats.

Training programs should cover various topics, including phishing awareness, secure password practices, social engineering, and best practices for secure system usage. Regular security awareness campaigns and simulated phishing exercises can help reinforce security practices and cultivate a culture of vigilance within the organization.

Additionally, custodians should provide specific training on digital asset-related security risks and best practices. This includes educating employees about the unique risks associated with digital assets, such as the potential for targeted attacks, the importance of secure custody practices, and the handling of private keys.

2.6.4 Continuous Risk Assessment and Audits

Custodians should conduct regular risk assessments and security audits to identify vulnerabilities, assess the effectiveness of security controls, and address any gaps or weaknesses in their security posture.

Risk assessments involve identifying and evaluating potential threats, vulnerabilities, and impacts to digital assets. This enables custodians to prioritize security initiatives, allocate resources effectively, and implement appropriate risk mitigation measures.

Security audits, conducted by internal or external experts, provide an independent evaluation of custodial practices and adherence to security standards. Audits can assess the effectiveness of security controls, review compliance with regulatory requirements, and identify areas for improvement. Custodians should ensure that audit reports are shared with relevant stakeholders to demonstrate transparency and accountability.

2.6.5 Collaboration and Information Sharing

Custodians should actively participate in industry collaborations and share information about security threats, vulnerabilities, and best practices. Collaboration with other custodians, industry associations, and regulatory bodies fosters the exchange of knowledge and insights, enabling custodians to stay informed about emerging threats and industry trends.

Information sharing platforms, such as threat intelligence networks or cybersecurity forums, facilitate the sharing of anonymized security incident data, indicators of compromise, and mitigation strategies. Custodians can leverage these platforms to gain valuable insights into emerging threats, enhance their incident response capabilities, and contribute to the collective defense against cyber threats.

In conclusion, custodians must implement robust cybersecurity measures to safeguard digital assets against cyber threats. Comprehensive security frameworks, secure storage and key management practices, ongoing education and training programs, continuous risk assessments, and collaboration are key elements of custodial best practices. By prioritizing cybersecurity, custodians can enhance the protection of digital assets and maintain the trust of asset owners in the rapidly evolving digital asset landscape.

2.7 The Importance of Asset Verification and Provenance

In the realm of digital asset custody, asset verification and provenance play a vital role in ensuring the integrity, authenticity, and traceability of assets. As digital assets gain prominence and adoption, the ability to verify the existence and ownership of assets becomes increasingly crucial. In this section, we will explore the significance of asset verification and provenance in the context of digital asset custody, highlighting the benefits they offer and the challenges they present.

2.7.1 Verifying Asset Authenticity

Verifying the authenticity of digital assets is a critical aspect of custodial services. Asset authenticity refers to confirming that the asset is genuine and has not been tampered with or counterfeited. This is particularly relevant for digital assets that can be easily replicated or manipulated.

To ensure asset authenticity, custodians must employ rigorous verification processes. This may involve conducting thorough due diligence on the asset issuer, reviewing relevant documentation and contracts, and assessing the asset's compliance with regulatory requirements. Additionally, custodians can leverage technologies such as cryptographic hashes, digital signatures, or unique identifiers to provide tamper-evident proofs of asset authenticity.

Asset authenticity verification also extends to the validation of asset metadata and associated information. Custodians should validate attributes such as asset type, quantity, ownership rights, and any other relevant details specified by the asset issuer. This validation process helps ensure that the asset being held in custody aligns with the intended characteristics and specifications.

2.7.2 Establishing Asset Provenance

Asset provenance refers to the ability to trace the history, origin, and ownership of an asset throughout its lifecycle. Provenance is particularly important in digital asset custody as it enables asset owners and custodians to establish a clear record of ownership, validate asset transfers, and demonstrate compliance with regulatory requirements.

Blockchain technology plays a crucial role in establishing asset provenance for many digital assets. The transparent and immutable nature of blockchain enables a verifiable record of all asset transactions and transfers. Asset owners and custodians can leverage blockchain-based ledgers to trace the complete history of an asset, including its creation, ownership changes, and any associated transactions.

For assets that do not operate on blockchain networks, custodians must establish robust documentation and record-keeping practices to maintain a comprehensive history of asset transfers and ownership. This may involve maintaining detailed transaction logs, securely storing asset-related documentation, and implementing robust data management systems.

2.7.3 Benefits of Asset Verification and Provenance

Asset verification and provenance offer several benefits to both custodians and asset owners. By ensuring asset authenticity, custodians can mitigate the risk of holding counterfeit or tampered assets. This enhances the overall trustworthiness of the custodial service and protects asset owners from potential fraud or loss.

Asset verification and provenance also contribute to regulatory compliance. Regulatory authorities often require custodians to demonstrate the legitimacy and traceability of assets. By establishing robust asset verification and provenance processes, custodians can meet these compliance requirements and demonstrate transparency and accountability to regulators and auditors.

Additionally, asset verification and provenance provide asset owners with peace of mind and confidence in the custody of their digital assets. The ability to verify the authenticity and trace the provenance of assets ensures that asset owners have a clear understanding of the assets being held in custody. This transparency and visibility enable asset owners to make informed decisions regarding their digital assets, including potential transfers, sales, or collateralization.

Asset verification and provenance also contribute to the broader ecosystem of digital assets. As the digital asset space matures, the ability to verify assets and establish provenance becomes increasingly important for wider adoption. Robust verification and provenance processes enhance market confidence, facilitate asset liquidity, and enable the development of secondary markets for digital assets.

2.7.4 Challenges in Asset Verification and Provenance

While asset verification and provenance are essential, custodians face various challenges in implementing robust processes. One key challenge is the lack of standardization in asset verification and provenance practices. The digital asset landscape is diverse, with various asset types, issuance platforms, and regulatory frameworks. Custodians must navigate these complexities and develop adaptable processes that align with the specific requirements of each asset.

Another challenge lies in verifying the authenticity and provenance of off-chain assets, such as real-world assets tokenized on a blockchain. Custodians must establish reliable mechanisms to link the digital representation of the asset to the physical asset itself, ensuring that the asset's characteristics and ownership rights are accurately reflected.

Interoperability between different blockchain networks and asset verification systems is another challenge. Digital assets may operate on different blockchains or utilize different verification mechanisms, making it difficult to establish a unified view of asset verification and provenance. Custodians must navigate these interoperability challenges to ensure a comprehensive and accurate representation of asset history and ownership.

Privacy considerations also come into play when dealing with asset verification and provenance. While transparency is a key aspect of establishing asset provenance, custodians must balance the need for transparency with data privacy requirements. Sensitive information, such as personal identifiable information (PII) or commercially sensitive details, must be handled with care to ensure compliance with data protection regulations.

2.7.5 Innovations and Future Directions

The field of asset verification and provenance is continually evolving, driven by technological advancements and regulatory developments. Innovations such as zero-knowledge proofs and privacy-preserving technologies aim to enhance privacy while enabling verifiable asset authenticity and provenance. These innovations provide opportunities for custodians to strike a balance between transparency and privacy.

Standardization efforts and industry collaborations are also underway to establish common frameworks for asset verification and provenance. These initiatives aim to streamline verification processes, enhance interoperability, and facilitate the exchange of verified asset information across different platforms and custodians. Custodians can actively engage in these industry discussions and contribute to the development of standardized practices.

Furthermore, emerging technologies such as Internet of Things (IoT) devices and artificial intelligence (AI) can play a role in asset verification and provenance. IoT devices can provide real-time data on physical assets, enabling custodians to verify the existence and condition of the underlying assets. AI-powered algorithms can analyze large datasets to identify patterns and anomalies, supporting the detection of fraudulent or counterfeit assets.

In conclusion, asset verification and provenance are essential aspects of digital asset custody. Robust asset verification processes and the establishment of asset provenance enable custodians to ensure the authenticity, integrity, and traceability of digital assets. By implementing robust practices, custodians can enhance trust, comply with regulatory requirements, and provide asset owners with the confidence that their digital assets are handled securely and transparently.

2.8 Auditing and Transparency in Digital Asset Custody

Auditing and transparency play a crucial role in the realm of digital asset custody. As custodians hold and manage valuable digital assets on behalf of asset owners, ensuring transparency and accountability is of paramount importance. In this section, we will explore the significance of auditing and transparency in digital asset custody, the benefits they offer, and the challenges they present.

2.8.1 The Importance of Auditing

Auditing is a critical process that allows custodians to assess the effectiveness of their internal controls, risk management practices, and compliance with regulatory requirements. Through regular audits, custodians can identify potential vulnerabilities, weaknesses, or non-compliance issues and take appropriate measures to address them.

Internal audits provide an independent evaluation of custodial operations and processes. They involve a comprehensive review of internal controls, custody procedures, security measures, and adherence to established policies and guidelines. Internal auditors assess the effectiveness of these controls and identify areas for improvement or enhancement.

External audits, conducted by independent auditing firms or regulatory bodies, further validate the custodian's compliance with regulatory requirements, industry standards, and best practices. External auditors review the custodian's systems, processes, and documentation to provide an objective assessment of the custodian's operations and controls.

Auditing also plays a vital role in establishing trust and confidence among asset owners and stakeholders. The existence of regular audits and the transparency of audit reports demonstrate the custodian's commitment to maintaining high standards of security, compliance, and operational integrity.

2.8.2 Enhancing Transparency

Transparency is a key element in digital asset custody as it fosters trust, accountability, and market confidence. Custodians must provide transparency to asset owners by offering clear visibility into their operations, security practices, and the management of digital assets.

Transparency can be achieved through various means, including regular reporting, disclosure of key metrics and performance indicators, and clear communication channels with asset owners. Custodians should provide detailed reports on custody activities, asset holdings, transaction histories, and any significant incidents or breaches. These reports should be easily accessible to asset owners and should clearly outline the custodian's adherence to security protocols, compliance with regulatory requirements, and the effectiveness of internal controls.

Transparency also extends to the disclosure of custody fees, fee structures, and any potential conflicts of interest. Asset owners rely on custodians to provide fair and transparent pricing models, ensuring they understand the costs associated with custody services and any additional fees they may incur.

Furthermore, custodians should maintain open lines of communication with asset owners, promptly addressing inquiries, concerns, or requests for information. This communication fosters trust and allows asset owners to actively participate in the custody process, knowing they have access to the necessary information to make informed decisions regarding their digital assets.

2.8.3 Benefits of Auditing and Transparency

Auditing and transparency provide several benefits to both custodians and asset owners. For custodians, regular audits and transparency demonstrate their commitment to maintaining the highest standards of security, compliance, and operational excellence. Audits help identify potential vulnerabilities or weaknesses in custody processes, allowing custodians to take proactive measures to strengthen their controls and mitigate risks. Transparency fosters trust and confidence among asset owners, helping custodians attract and retain clients in the competitive digital asset custody landscape.

For asset owners, auditing and transparency offer assurance that their digital assets are being managed in a secure and compliant manner. The availability of audit reports and transparent reporting allows asset owners to assess the custodian's operational integrity, compliance with regulatory requirements, and adherence to industry best practices. This transparency enables asset owners to make informed decisions when selecting a custodian and provides a basis for ongoing monitoring of custodial activities.

Auditing and transparency also contribute to the overall stability and integrity of the digital asset ecosystem. As the digital asset industry continues to evolve, regulatory frameworks are being established to ensure market transparency and protect investor interests. Custodians that demonstrate a commitment to auditing and transparency contribute to the development of a robust and well-regulated digital asset ecosystem.

2.8.4 Challenges in Auditing and Transparency

Auditing and transparency in digital asset custody come with their own set of challenges. One of the primary challenges is the evolving nature of the digital asset landscape. The rapid pace of technological advancements and the emergence of new asset classes make it challenging for auditors to keep up with the complexity and uniqueness of digital asset custody practices. Auditors must possess a deep understanding of digital assets, blockchain technology, and relevant regulatory requirements to effectively evaluate custodial operations.

Another challenge lies in striking a balance between transparency and data privacy. While transparency is essential for fostering trust, custodians must also ensure the protection of sensitive client data and comply with data protection regulations. Implementing robust data privacy measures, such as encryption, access controls, and anonymization, helps custodians maintain confidentiality while providing the necessary transparency.

Additionally, ensuring the consistency and comparability of audit reports across custodians can be challenging. The lack of standardized reporting frameworks and metrics in the digital asset custody space makes it difficult for asset owners and regulators to assess and compare the performance and security measures of different custodians. Collaborative efforts among industry participants, regulators, and standard-setting bodies are necessary to establish common reporting frameworks that enable meaningful transparency and benchmarking

2.8.5 Future Directions in Auditing and Transparency

The field of auditing and transparency in digital asset custody is evolving to address the unique challenges and opportunities presented by digital assets. Technological innovations, such as blockchain-based audit trails and smart contracts, hold promise for enhancing the transparency and efficiency of auditing processes. These technologies enable real-time monitoring of custodial activities, automated verification of transaction records, and the creation of immutable audit trails.

Standard-setting bodies and industry associations are also working towards developing common frameworks and best practices for auditing and transparency in digital asset custody. Collaborative initiatives aim to establish industry-wide standards, reporting requirements, and performance benchmarks that promote consistency, comparability, and increased transparency across custodial services.

Furthermore, the integration of emerging technologies, such as artificial intelligence (AI) and machine learning, into auditing processes can enhance the effectiveness and efficiency of audits. AI-powered analytics tools can analyze large volumes of data, identify patterns, and detect anomalies, supporting auditors in the identification of potential risks or non-compliance issues.

In conclusion, auditing and transparency are essential components of digital asset custody. Regular audits and transparent reporting demonstrate a custodian's commitment to security, compliance, and operational integrity. By prioritizing auditing and transparency, custodians can build trust, attract and retain clients, and contribute to the development of a robust and transparent digital asset ecosystem.

2.10 The Emergence of Institutional Custodianship

Institutional custodianship has emerged as a critical component in the world of digital asset custody. As digital assets gain recognition and adoption among institutional investors, the need for specialized custodial services tailored to their unique requirements has become increasingly apparent. In this section, we will explore the emergence of institutional custodianship, its significance in the digital asset landscape, and the benefits it offers.

2.10.1 Understanding Institutional Custodianship

Institutional custodianship refers to the provision of custodial services specifically designed for institutional investors. Institutional investors, such as hedge funds, asset managers, pension funds, and family offices, have distinct requirements when it comes to managing and safeguarding their digital assets.

Institutional custodians are custodial service providers that cater to the needs of institutional investors. They offer a range of services, including secure storage, asset administration, risk management, compliance support, reporting, and specialized client support. Institutional custodians understand the complexities and regulatory considerations specific to institutional investors, providing them with tailored solutions and expertise.

2.10.2 The Significance of Institutional Custodianship

The emergence of institutional custodianship is a significant development in the digital asset landscape for several reasons. Firstly, institutional investors bring substantial capital and credibility to the digital asset space. Their entry into the market not only contributes to increased liquidity and market maturity but also promotes wider adoption and acceptance of digital assets as an asset class.

Secondly, institutional investors have unique requirements and expectations when it comes to custody services. They demand robust security measures, sophisticated risk management frameworks, comprehensive reporting capabilities, and regulatory compliance support. Institutional custodians are specifically positioned to address these needs, providing a level of expertise and service tailored to the expectations of institutional investors.

Furthermore, the involvement of institutional custodians enhances market trust and transparency. Institutional investors often have rigorous due diligence processes and compliance requirements, which custodians must meet to secure their business. By working with reputable institutional custodians, investors can have confidence in the security and integrity of their digital assets.

2.10.3 Benefits of Institutional Custodianship

Institutional custodianship offers several benefits to both institutional investors and the broader digital asset ecosystem. For institutional investors, partnering with institutional custodians provides access to specialized expertise and resources. These custodians have a deep understanding of institutional investors' unique requirements and can tailor their services to meet their specific needs. This includes offering sophisticated risk management tools, compliance support, and reporting capabilities that align with institutional standards.

Institutional custodians also bring a higher level of security and risk mitigation to the table. They implement stringent security protocols, including multi-signature wallets, cold storage solutions, and comprehensive cybersecurity measures, to protect digital assets from unauthorized access and theft. Institutional investors can leverage these robust security measures to mitigate risks associated with holding and managing digital assets.

Additionally, institutional custodians often offer regulatory compliance support. They stay updated on evolving regulatory frameworks and ensure that their custodial practices align with the latest requirements. This helps institutional investors navigate the complex regulatory landscape surrounding digital assets, reducing compliance risks and ensuring adherence to regulatory obligations.

The involvement of institutional custodians also enhances the overall credibility and reputation of the digital asset ecosystem. Their rigorous due diligence processes, comprehensive reporting capabilities, and adherence to industry best practices contribute to increased transparency and market trust. This, in turn, attracts additional institutional investors and fosters the development of a well-regulated and robust digital asset market.

2.10.4 Challenges in Institutional Custodianship

While institutional custodianship offers significant benefits, there are challenges to consider. One challenge is the evolving regulatory landscape surrounding digital assets. Regulatory frameworks vary across jurisdictions, and custodians must navigate these complexities to ensure compliance with relevant regulations. Institutional custodians need to stay updated on regulatory changes and adapt their custodial practices accordingly.

Another challenge is scalability. As the demand for institutional custodial services increases, custodians must be prepared to scale their operations to meet the growing needs of institutional investors. This includes expanding their infrastructure, implementing advanced technologies, and enhancing their operational capabilities to handle large volumes of digital assets effectively.

Additionally, there is a need for continued innovation in institutional custodianship. As the digital asset landscape evolves, custodians must stay ahead of emerging trends and technologies to provide cutting-edge solutions to institutional investors. This includes exploring advancements such as decentralized finance (DeFi), tokenization, and interoperability to meet the evolving demands of institutional clients.

2.10.5 Conclusion and Future Outlook

The emergence of institutional custodianship is a significant development in the digital asset industry. Institutional investors bring capital, credibility, and stringent requirements to the market, driving the need for specialized custodial services. Institutional custodians cater to these requirements, offering tailored solutions, robust security measures, regulatory compliance support, and expertise specific to institutional investors.

The involvement of institutional custodians contributes to the maturation and acceptance of digital assets as an asset class. Their presence enhances market transparency, credibility, and trust, attracting additional institutional investors and promoting wider adoption of digital assets. As the digital asset industry continues to evolve, institutional custodians will play a crucial role in meeting the unique needs of institutional investors and driving the growth of the ecosystem.

2.11 Custodial Services for Decentralized Finance (DeFi) Assets

The emergence of decentralized finance (DeFi) has revolutionized the financial landscape by offering innovative and decentralized financial products and services. With the rapid growth of DeFi assets, the need for secure and reliable custodial services tailored to these unique digital assets has become increasingly important. In this section, we will explore the role of custodial services in managing DeFi assets, the challenges they face, and the benefits they offer.

2.11.1 Understanding DeFi Assets

DeFi assets refer to digital assets that operate within decentralized financial ecosystems built on blockchain technology. These assets include cryptocurrencies, tokens, and other digital representations of value that facilitate various financial activities such as lending, borrowing, yield farming, decentralized exchanges, and more.

Unlike traditional financial systems, DeFi assets operate without intermediaries or central authorities. They rely on smart contracts and decentralized protocols to execute transactions, manage assets, and enforce rules. This decentralized nature provides users with increased control over their funds and eliminates the need for traditional financial intermediaries.

2.11.2 The Role of Custodial Services in DeFi

While DeFi assets aim to provide users with greater autonomy and control over their funds, there is still a need for custodial services to facilitate secure storage, manage private keys, and offer additional services to institutional and individual investors.

Custodial services for DeFi assets play a crucial role in addressing the unique challenges and risks associated with decentralized finance. Custodians provide a bridge between traditional financial institutions and the decentralized world by offering secure storage solutions, asset administration, risk management, and compliance support.

One of the key responsibilities of custodial services in the DeFi space is secure storage. Custodians employ robust security measures such as hardware wallets, multi-signature wallets, and secure vaults to protect private keys and digital assets from unauthorized access or theft. By securely storing private keys on behalf of users, custodians mitigate the risk of loss or compromise due to user errors or vulnerabilities in personal wallets.

Custodial services also assist in managing the complexities of interacting with decentralized protocols and executing transactions on behalf of clients. They ensure that DeFi assets are held securely and that users can access and utilize their assets efficiently within the decentralized ecosystem. Additionally, custodians help users navigate the evolving DeFi landscape, offering guidance on investment strategies, portfolio management, and risk assessment.

Furthermore, custodians in the DeFi space can provide compliance support and reporting services. Given the increasing scrutiny and regulatory requirements in the digital asset space, custodians ensure that users and investors adhere to applicable regulations, including anti-money laundering (AML) and know-your-customer (KYC) requirements. Custodians can implement robust compliance frameworks, monitor transactions for suspicious activities, and generate necessary reports to demonstrate compliance to regulatory authorities.

2.11.3 Challenges in Custodial Services for DeFi Assets

Custodial services for DeFi assets come with their own set of challenges. One of the primary challenges is the evolving nature of the DeFi ecosystem. DeFi protocols and platforms undergo rapid innovation and iteration, introducing new asset classes, complex smart contract structures, and evolving security risks. Custodians need to continually adapt and stay ahead of these changes to ensure the secure management of DeFi assets.

Interoperability is another challenge in the DeFi space. With multiple protocols and platforms operating independently, custodians must navigate interoperability challenges to provide comprehensive custody services. Interoperability solutions, such as cross-chain bridges and decentralized liquidity protocols, are being developed to address this challenge, allowing custodians to securely manage assets across different blockchain networks.

Moreover, due to the decentralized nature of DeFi, users maintain control over their private keys and assets. This poses challenges for custodians as they need to strike a balance between providing secure custody services while respecting user autonomy. Custodians must implement robust security measures to safeguard assets, educate users about best practices for maintaining control over their private keys, and develop secure mechanisms for user interactions.

2.11.4 Benefits of Custodial Services for DeFi Assets

Custodial services for DeFi assets offer several benefits to users, investors, and the broader DeFi ecosystem. One of the primary benefits is enhanced security. Custodians employ rigorous security measures, such as multi-layered authentication, hardware wallets, and comprehensive cybersecurity protocols, to protect assets from unauthorized access, hacks, and theft. This provides users with peace of mind knowing that their assets are held and managed by trusted custodians.

Custodial services also provide convenience and ease of use. DeFi can be complex, particularly for users unfamiliar with blockchain technology and smart contracts. Custodians simplify the user experience by offering intuitive interfaces, simplified asset management, and assistance with transaction execution. This enables a broader range of users to participate in DeFi activities, expanding the accessibility and adoption of decentralized finance.

Additionally, custodians in the DeFi space can offer institutional-grade services and compliance support. Institutional investors often require robust risk management frameworks, regulatory compliance support, and comprehensive reporting capabilities. Custodians can provide these services, helping institutional investors navigate the unique challenges and regulatory considerations of the DeFi space.

Furthermore, custodial services contribute to the overall credibility and trustworthiness of the DeFi ecosystem. By implementing rigorous security measures, ensuring compliance with regulatory requirements, and offering transparent reporting, custodians enhance market confidence and attract a broader range of participants, including institutional investors and traditional financial institutions.

2.11.5 Conclusion and Future Outlook

Custodial services for DeFi assets play a vital role in the evolving landscape of decentralized finance. They provide secure storage, risk management, compliance support, and additional services that bridge the gap between traditional financial institutions and the decentralized world. Custodians enable users to securely manage and utilize their assets within the DeFi ecosystem, enhancing convenience, security, and accessibility.

As the DeFi space continues to expand and mature, custodial services will play an increasingly important role in addressing the unique challenges and risks associated with decentralized finance. Custodians must adapt to the evolving DeFi ecosystem, navigate interoperability challenges, and provide innovative solutions to meet the needs of users and investors.

3 Technological Fundamentals for Digital Asset Custody

3.1 Introduction to Technological Fundamentals

As we delve into the realm of digital asset custody, it's essential to understand the technological fundamentals that underpin this landscape. The exciting world of digital assets, powered by groundbreaking technologies like blockchain and cryptography, has rewritten the rule book on how we manage, store, and secure wealth. In this section, we'll provide a broad overview of the key technological principles that form the foundation of digital asset custody.

3.1.1 The Dawn of Digital Assets

Since the launch of Bitcoin in 2009, the world has been introduced to an entirely new form of value storage and transfer: digital assets. These assets, represented digitally and managed on a variety of platforms, have brought about an unprecedented shift in the global financial ecosystem. They encompass a wide range of assets, including cryptocurrencies like Bitcoin and Ethereum, tokens representing real-world assets, non-fungible tokens (NFTs), and much more.

3.1.2 Blockchain: The Backbone of Digital Assets

The underlying technology behind the operation and management of these digital assets is blockchain. A blockchain is a type of distributed ledger, where data is stored across multiple computers globally in a highly secure, transparent, and immutable manner. The unique attributes of blockchain technology, such as decentralization and security, make it a perfect fit for facilitating and recording digital asset transactions.

3.1.3 The Role of Cryptography

Cryptography plays a pivotal role in the secure operation of digital assets. It is the science of encoding and decoding information to prevent unauthorized access. In digital asset custody, cryptographic techniques are used to secure transactions, validate asset ownership, and protect the integrity of assets. The most common application of cryptography in this space is through cryptographic keys - pairs of private and public keys that are used to sign and verify transactions.

Traditional vs DA Custodians schema

3.1.4 Secure Storage Solutions: Wallets

One of the most significant technological aspects of digital asset custody is the storage solution, often referred to as a wallet. Wallets can be software-based (hot wallets) or hardware-based (cold wallets). Hot wallets are connected to the internet and provide easy access and transaction capabilities, while cold wallets are offline storage devices that offer enhanced security by keeping assets away from potential online threats.

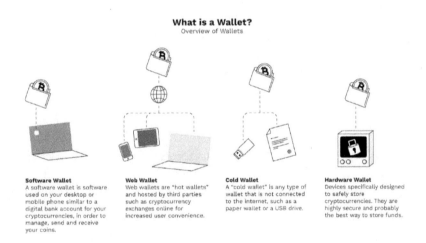

3.1.5 The Increasing Complexity: Smart Contracts and DeFi

The digital asset custody landscape is constantly evolving, with emerging technologies such as smart contracts and decentralized finance (DeFi) adding layers of complexity. Smart contracts are programmable contracts that automatically execute when predefined conditions are met, providing increased efficiency and security. Meanwhile, DeFi represents a spectrum of financial applications built on blockchain networks, expanding the utility and scope of digital assets.

3.1.6 Emphasizing Interoperability

Interoperability - the ability of different blockchain networks to work together seamlessly - is another key technological aspect. With a myriad of blockchain networks supporting various digital assets, the need for cross-chain solutions and interoperable platforms becomes crucial for a comprehensive and efficient digital asset custody solution.

3.1.7 The Criticality of Privacy and Anonymity

Lastly, the principles of privacy and anonymity are central to many digital asset platforms. While transparency is a hallmark of blockchain technology, preserving user privacy and ensuring secure, anonymous transactions is a key requirement for many users and a major focus of various digital asset networks.

This section serves as the introduction to the profound world of technology that empowers digital asset custody. As we progress further into this chapter, each of these concepts will be explored in detail, providing a comprehensive understanding of the technological fundamentals in digital asset custody. By grasping these core concepts, we can better appreciate the intricacies, challenges, and innovations that make up the vibrant, continuously evolving landscape of digital asset custody.

3.2 Blockchain Technology: The Foundation of Digital Asset Custody

Blockchain technology is undeniably the backbone of digital asset custody, providing the fundamental infrastructure that allows digital assets to exist, transact, and be stored securely. To fully understand digital asset custody, we must first understand the basics of blockchain technology, its functionalities, and its implications for digital asset management.

3.2.1 Understanding Blockchain Technology

At its core, a blockchain is a type of distributed ledger that records transactions across numerous computers so that any involved record cannot be altered retroactively, without the modification of all subsequent blocks. This approach offers unmatched security and transparency, making it an ideal infrastructure for the digital asset world.

The transactions are grouped in blocks, recorded one after the other in a chronological manner forming a chain - hence, the name "blockchain". Each block contains a cryptographic hash of the previous one, timestamp, and transaction data. This unique structure ensures that once data is recorded in a block, it is virtually impossible to change it, establishing the immutability feature of blockchain.

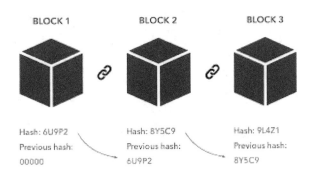

Blockchain schema

3.2.2 Decentralization: A Key Principle

One of the fundamental principles of blockchain technology is decentralization. Unlike traditional centralized databases where a single entity has control over the entire database, in a blockchain, control is distributed among a network of nodes or computers. This characteristic reduces the risk of single-point failures and attacks, increasing the security and resilience of the network.

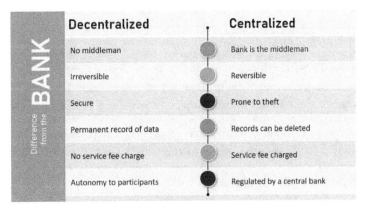

Blockchain for finance

3.2.3 Consensus Mechanisms

Blockchain networks operate using consensus mechanisms to validate transactions and add new blocks to the chain. These mechanisms are protocols that ensure all nodes in the network agree on the content of the blockchain. Some of the most common consensus mechanisms include Proof of Work (PoW) and Proof of Stake (PoS), each with its unique characteristics and security considerations.

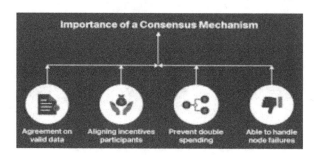

Why a consensus mechanism?

3.2.4 Blockchain and Digital Assets

The advent of blockchain technology has made digital assets possible. Digital assets, such as cryptocurrencies, utilize blockchain technology for the creation (also known as minting), transaction, and storage of these assets. For instance, Bitcoin operates on a PoW blockchain where miners solve complex mathematical problems to add new blocks to the chain, and Ethereum is transitioning to a PoS blockchain to improve scalability and energy efficiency.

3.2.5 Role of Blockchain in Digital Asset Custody

In the context of digital asset custody, blockchain serves as the foundational technology enabling the secure management and storage of digital assets. The immutable and transparent nature of blockchain allows for the clear tracking and recording of digital asset transactions, vital for audits and regulatory compliance.

Moreover, blockchain wallets, which are essentially cryptographic key pairs, provide secure storage for digital assets. The public key allows others to send assets to the wallet, while the private key enables the owner to access and manage their assets.

3.2.6 Different Types of Blockchains

It's important to note that not all blockchains are the same. We have public blockchains like Bitcoin and Ethereum, where anyone can participate. There are also private blockchains where participation is restricted, often used by businesses for inter-organizational transactions. Furthermore, there are consortium blockchains where multiple organizations manage the network collectively. Each type of blockchain has its specific use cases, benefits, and security considerations.

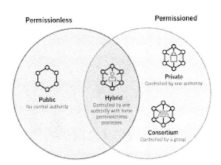

Types of blockchains

3.2.7 Future Trends: Blockchain and Beyond

Blockchain continues to evolve, with new developments such as sharding and layer 2 solutions aimed at solving scalability issues. Also, interoperable blockchains that can communicate and transact with one another are gaining momentum, opening new possibilities for digital asset management.

Understanding the foundations of blockchain technology, its benefits, challenges, and future trends is vital to grasp the intricacies of digital asset custody fully. With its unprecedented security, transparency, and immutability, blockchain technology is undoubtedly the driving force behind digital asset custody.

3.3 Public and Private Key Cryptography: Ensuring Secure Transactions

Public and private key cryptography, also known as asymmetric cryptography, is a vital element of secure digital asset transactions. The security, privacy, and unique ownership attributes that define digital assets are largely a result of this cryptographic technique. This section will delve into the nuts and bolts of public and private key cryptography, explaining its role, functions, and the critical part it plays in the world of digital asset custody.

3.3.1 Understanding Asymmetric Cryptography

Asymmetric cryptography is a cryptographic system that uses pairs of keys: public keys, which may be disseminated widely, and private keys, which are known only to the owner. In digital asset transactions, the public key is used to encrypt the transaction, and the corresponding private key is used to decrypt it. This fundamental system is the bedrock of secure digital asset transactions, allowing users to verify the authenticity of a transaction without exposing their private key.

3.3.2 Generating Public and Private Keys

The process of generating a public-private key pair is rooted in complex mathematical algorithms. In the case of Bitcoin and many other digital assets, elliptic curve cryptography (ECC) is used. ECC is an approach to public key cryptography based on the algebraic structure of elliptic curves over finite fields. The details of ECC can be highly technical, but in essence, it provides a robust foundation for security due to the computational difficulty of the discrete logarithm problem on which it is based.

3.3.3 How Key Pairs Facilitate Transactions

When a transaction is made in the digital asset world, the sender creates a message (the transaction), then encrypts it using the receiver's public key. This encrypted transaction is broadcast to the network for validation. It can only be decrypted by the receiver's private key, ensuring the secure transmission of assets. Furthermore, the sender often signs the transaction with their private key, providing a cryptographic proof of the origin of the transaction, a process known as digital signing. The combination of these cryptographic techniques ensures both the secure transmission of assets and the authenticity of transactions.

3.3.4 Public and Private Keys: Securing Digital Asset Wallets

Public and private keys are also crucial components of digital asset wallets. A wallet can be thought of as a pair of a private key and the corresponding public key (or address). The public key or address is used to receive funds, while the private key is used to sign transactions to spend the assets. The security of a wallet, therefore, is entirely dependent on the secrecy and secure management of the private key.

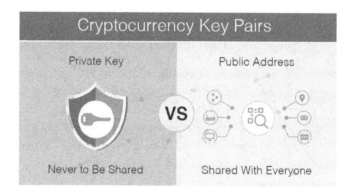

Public and Private Keys

3.3.5 Key Management: Safeguarding Private Keys

Proper key management is one of the most critical aspects of digital asset custody. Private keys must be kept secret, as anyone with access to a private key can sign transactions and potentially access the assets the key controls. If a private key is lost, the assets are effectively lost as well, as there is no way to regenerate the key. Therefore, private key management techniques, such as secure key storage, key backup, key recovery, and key disposal, are fundamental to digital asset custody.

3.3.6 Challenges of Public and Private Key Cryptography

While public and private key cryptography provides a strong foundation for secure transactions and asset management, it also presents challenges. One of the primary challenges is the complexity of managing private keys, especially for novices. Furthermore, the irreversible nature of digital asset transactions can lead to significant losses if a user loses access to their private keys or if they are stolen.

3.3.7 Addressing Challenges: Custodial Solutions

Custodial solutions are aimed at addressing these challenges, providing users with secure management and backup of their private keys, often using specialized hardware and software solutions. By providing expert management of private keys, custodial services can significantly enhance the security and ease of use of digital assets for a wide range of users.

3.3.8 Future Trends: Multi-Signature, Hierarchical Deterministic Wallets and More

Future trends in the realm of public and private key cryptography include the increased use of multi-signature wallets and hierarchical deterministic (HD) wallets. Multi-signature wallets require multiple private keys to authorize a transaction, providing an additional layer of security. HD wallets allow for the creation of a tree of key pairs from a single seed, simplifying key management while maintaining a high level of security.

3.3.9 Conclusion: The Indispensable Role of Public and Private Key Cryptography

Public and private key cryptography is one of the cornerstone technologies of digital assets, enabling the secure, private, and unique ownership characteristics that set digital assets apart. Understanding the role and function of public and private key cryptography is crucial for anyone seeking to grasp the intricacies of digital asset custody.

3.4 Multi-Signature Wallets: Enhancing Security and Access Control

As digital assets continue to gain prominence, safeguarding them is of paramount importance. In the context of secure storage and transaction authorizations, multi-signature wallets have emerged as an effective solution. They offer an added layer of security and more versatile access control, making them ideal for many digital asset custody scenarios. This section delves into multi-signature wallets, discussing their workings, advantages, use-cases, and their increasing significance in digital asset custody.

3.4.1 Understanding Multi-Signature Wallets

A multi-signature wallet, also known as a multisig wallet, is a digital wallet that requires multiple signatures to authorize a digital asset transaction. In the traditional banking system, this would be akin to a safety deposit box that requires two or more keys to open. In the context of digital assets, these "keys" are cryptographic signatures derived from distinct private keys.

Multi-signature scheme

3.4.2 Setting Up Multi-Signature Wallets

Setting up a multisig wallet typically involves defining the total number of keys and how many keys are needed to sign a transaction (also known as the M-of-N scheme, where M are the required signatures and N is the total number of keys). A 2-of-3 scheme, for instance, means that there are three keys in total, and any two are required to authorize a transaction. This setup can be customized according to the user's specific requirements for security and access control.

3.4.3 Advantages of Multi-Signature Wallets

Multi-signature wallets offer several advantages over traditional single-key wallets. The requirement for multiple signatures makes them highly resistant to single point failures or attacks. If one key is compromised, the assets in the wallet remain secure as the attacker cannot meet the signature requirement.

Furthermore, multi-signature wallets enable more flexible and robust access control, making them suitable for organizations or situations where multiple parties need to authorize transactions. They also provide an inherent backup feature - even if one key is lost, the remaining keys can access and move the assets.

3.4.4 Use Cases of Multi-Signature Wallets

Multi-signature wallets have numerous practical applications. They're often used by businesses dealing with digital assets, where corporate governance rules may require multiple approvals for transactions. They're also useful for individual users wanting to enhance security, share control of assets, or implement a backup mechanism for their private keys. Furthermore, multisig wallets can facilitate trustless escrow services, where a neutral third party can arbitrate disputes without having full control of the assets.

3.4.5 Implementing Multi-Signature Wallets

Several digital asset platforms support multi-signature wallets. Bitcoin was the first to introduce native multi-signature support, and now many other digital asset platforms, including Ethereum, offer multisig functionalities. Some platforms also offer smart contract-based multisig wallets, adding programmability and versatility to the traditional multisig concept.

3.4.6 Challenges and Considerations

While multi-signature wallets provide increased security and flexibility, they also introduce added complexity. Managing multiple keys and coordinating signatures can be challenging, especially for less tech-savvy users. Moreover, the security of a multisig wallet is heavily dependent on secure key management practices. All parties involved must secure their keys properly to prevent any compromise.

3.4.7 Future of Multi-Signature Wallets

As digital assets continue to mature and become more mainstream, the adoption of multi-signature wallets is expected to rise. Innovations are also on the horizon, with advancements in smart contracts enabling more complex and flexible multisig setups. In the evolving landscape of digital asset custody, multi-signature wallets will undoubtedly play a critical role.

In summary, multi-signature wallets offer an effective mechanism to enhance the security and access control of digital asset custody. By requiring multiple signatures to authorize transactions, they provide resistance against single point failures and attacks, making them an integral component of any robust digital asset custody solution.

3.4.8 MPC Security: questions to ask your wallet provider.

In the realm of digital assets and blockchain-driven solutions, ensuring security is of paramount importance for organizations worldwide. While numerous providers of multi-party computation (MPC) make bold claims about offering top-notch security and service, what truly distinguishes them is the underlying cryptographic evidence and infrastructure.

Considering the severe repercussions that can arise from a security breach, it is essential to make well-informed decisions when evaluating an MPC wallet provider. Whether you are new to the world of cryptocurrency or already have an established product with an MPC wallet provider, asking these questions can help you initiate a meaningful discussion about MPC security.

1. Have you constructed a zero-trust architecture for your MPC protocol?

The most effective defense against cybercriminals involves employing a multi-layered security approach that can provide redundancy in case one of the security controls fails. There is no magic solution for security, so inquire about the various security layers and hardware defenses that your provider has implemented to safeguard each potential vulnerability. The objective is to eliminate dependence on a single security technology.

2. Are you up-to-date with the latest MPC algorithms, and do you utilize an open-source MPC protocol?

Numerous peer-reviewed MPC algorithms, such as GG-20, MPC-CMP, and MPC-CMPGG, are available today. Verify whether your wallet provider employs an MPC protocol that has undergone peer review and comprehensive auditing before integrating it into your product or offering it to customers.

Additionally, determine if the MPC protocol is open source, enabling you, as a customer, to scrutinize or have it reviewed by a third party. Open-sourcing the code fosters transparency and attracts a community of users, researchers, and developers, facilitating the collective advancement of software security.

3. *Does your implementation undergo audits by reputable third-party security firms? Ascertain whether your MPC provider invites third-party security companies to review the implementation of the MPC protocol you are utilizing, as well as its underlying cryptography. How frequently are these audits conducted? Are they performed regularly or only when significant changes occur?*

Third-party audits provide an objective perspective, validate claims, and challenge fundamental assumptions that your MPC provider might overlook, ensuring both security and credibility. Regularly undergoing audits is considered a best practice for any service provider, as they can expose vulnerabilities in the code, infrastructure, and critical operating systems of a protocol – including potential weaknesses among platform employees.

4. *How are key shares created, distributed, and stored?*

Inquire about where shared keys are stored, how they are stored, and what policies and procedures govern access to these keys. As a best practice, MPC key shares should be distributed among two or more organizations, with a high level of segregation between networking infrastructures and access control for each share.

Merely distributing MPC shares across multiple locations within a single organization – even if physically distant from one another – may not be sufficient to deter hackers. A more robust solution involves distributing MPC across multiple organizations that do not share servers or infrastructure.

For instance, one approach is to store a key share with an enterprise cloud provider. Some providers, for example, stores users' MPC shares within SGX hardware-isolated enclaves hosted by two distinct cloud providers: Microsoft Azure and IBM Cloud. In all cases, key shares are distributed in such a way that no single entity (including Fireblocks, the customer, or any individual cloud provider) can access the complete key.

5. *Do you have an in-house cryptography team to address potential vulnerabilities or attacks?*

Having an in-house cryptography team is crucial for ensuring the correct deployment of cryptographic protocols. These teams possess the knowledge and expertise to identify and resolve vulnerabilities promptly, ensuring the safety and security of your funds. If your chosen MPC wallet provider does not have a cryptography team dedicated to managing the security of its wallet infrastructure and proactively communicating risks to you, it should raise concerns.

6. *Find out what their incident response strategy or communication plan entails in the event that a vulnerability or attack is identified. How do they plan to communicate with internal security operations and customers?*

By being aware of your vendor's security status, you can ensure smooth business operations without potential disruptions. It is important to maintain open communication channels to relay potential vulnerabilities to the cryptography ecosystem. It is also essential to engage in transparent dialogues with their chosen MPC wallet providers to ensure visibility and alignment in terms of security measures.

3.5 Hardware Wallets: Physical Security for Digital Assets

As the value and adoption of digital assets continue to surge, securing these valuable assets becomes of paramount importance. While software wallets offer convenience and accessibility, they are inherently susceptible to online threats. In contrast, hardware wallets provide an innovative and robust solution by introducing physical security measures. In this section, we will explore hardware wallets, their working principles, advantages, and their role in bolstering the security of digital asset custody.

3.5.1 Understanding Hardware Wallets

A hardware wallet is a physical device designed specifically to store digital assets securely. It operates offline, meaning it remains disconnected from the internet when generating and signing transactions, making it impervious to online attacks and vulnerabilities. The core idea behind hardware wallets is to keep the private keys that control digital assets away from potential online threats, significantly reducing the risk of unauthorized access and asset theft.

3.5.2 How Hardware Wallets Work

Hardware wallets typically come with an embedded secure element, which is a tamper-resistant chip responsible for generating and storing private keys. These keys never leave the secure environment of the chip, ensuring that they are protected from external threats. When initiating a transaction, the hardware wallet displays the transaction details on its screen and requires user confirmation through physical button presses. Only then does the device sign the transaction and produce a unique digital signature, which is then sent to the network.

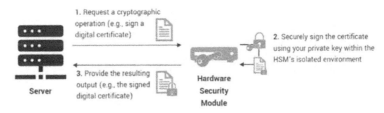

HSM scheme

3.5.3 Advantages of Hardware Wallets

Hardware wallets offer numerous advantages that make them an attractive choice for secure digital asset custody:

- Enhanced Security: The physical separation from the internet and the secure element's tamper-resistant design make hardware wallets highly secure against hacking attempts.
- Protection Against Phishing Attacks: Hardware wallets eliminate the risk of phishing attacks since the user must physically confirm transactions on the device.
- Versatile Asset Support: Many hardware wallets support a wide range of digital assets, providing a convenient single solution for managing different cryptocurrencies.
- Backup and Recovery: Hardware wallets offer straightforward backup and recovery procedures, ensuring that users can restore their assets if the device is lost or damaged.

- User-Friendly Interface: Most hardware wallets are designed with user-friendly interfaces, making them accessible to both tech-savvy and novice users.

3.5.4 Types of Hardware Wallets

There are two primary types of hardware wallets:

- USB-based Hardware Wallets: These wallets connect to a computer or smartphone via USB. They are compact, portable, and convenient for frequent transactions.
- Smartcard-based Hardware Wallets: These wallets resemble credit cards and have a small display and physical buttons for transaction confirmation. They are often used for contactless payments and offer additional physical protection.

3.5.5 Setting Up and Using Hardware Wallets

Setting up a hardware wallet typically involves initializing the device, generating a seed phrase (a backup of the wallet), and choosing a secure PIN. Once set up, the device can be used to send and receive digital assets securely. It's crucial to follow the manufacturer's guidelines and store the seed phrase securely offline as it is the key to recovering the wallet if needed.

3.5.6 Challenges and Considerations

While hardware wallets offer a high level of security, they are not entirely without challenges. One potential concern is the physical loss or damage of the device. Users must take precautions to store their hardware wallet safely, as a lost or damaged device can result in the loss of access to their digital assets. Additionally, users must ensure they purchase hardware wallets from reputable sources to avoid potential counterfeit devices.

3.5.7 Future of Hardware Wallets

As the digital asset industry continues to evolve, hardware wallet technology is expected to advance as well. We can anticipate improvements in usability, design, and compatibility with various digital asset protocols. Additionally, hardware wallets are likely to integrate with other security measures, such as biometric authentication, to further enhance their robustness.

In conclusion, hardware wallets represent a crucial component of digital asset custody, providing a physical layer of security to safeguard valuable digital assets. With their offline operation and tamper-resistant secure elements, hardware wallets significantly mitigate the risks associated with online threats, making them a preferred choice for individuals and organizations seeking top-tier security for their digital asset holdings.

3.6 Cold Storage Solutions: Safeguarding Assets Offline

The advent of digital assets brings unique challenges concerning safe storage. One of the most trusted methods for long-term, secure digital asset storage is the use of cold storage solutions. These solutions involve storing digital assets offline, away from potential online threats. This section explores cold storage, the benefits, the different types, and their crucial role in digital asset custody. We'll also delve into practical examples of its implementation.

3.6.1 Understanding Cold Storage

At its core, cold storage refers to any method of storing digital assets in a way that is not connected to the internet. By keeping assets offline, cold storage mitigates risks such as hacking, phishing, and other online threats. It's the digital equivalent of a physical safe deposit box, providing a high level of security for digital assets.

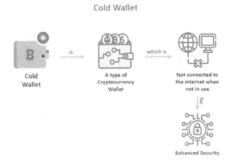

Cold wallet scheme

3.6.2 The Case for Cold Storage

With digital assets, securing private keys—the cryptographic strings that allow you to access and manage your digital assets—is paramount. If a malicious actor obtains your private keys, they can access and transfer your digital assets, resulting in a loss. Cold storage keeps these private keys offline, making them inaccessible to hackers who typically exploit internet connections to steal valuable information.

3.6.3 Types of Cold Storage Solutions

There are several methods of cold storage, each offering its own balance of security, convenience, and cost:

- Hardware Wallets: As discussed in Section 3.5, hardware wallets are physical devices that store users' private keys offline on a secure chip. They offer a high level of security and are easy to use, making them suitable for both individuals and institutions.
- Paper Wallets: A paper wallet is a document that contains a public address for receiving assets and a private key. The document is often printed with QR codes for easy scanning. Paper wallets are inexpensive and secure if created and stored properly. However, they can be damaged or lost, and are therefore often laminated or stored in a safe place.

- Metal Wallets: These are similar to paper wallets but are designed to be fireproof, waterproof, and shockproof. Users often etch or engrave their private keys or seed phrases onto pieces of metal.
- Air-gapped Computers: An air-gapped computer is never connected to the internet, providing a secure environment for generating and storing private keys. Transactions can be signed on the air-gapped computer and then transferred to an online device for broadcasting to the network.
- Cryptocurrency Safes: High-end solutions, such as cryptocurrency safes, store private keys on encrypted drives and utilize secure hardware modules for signing transactions. They are usually tamper-proof and require multi-factor authentication.

3.6.4 Implementing Cold Storage Solutions: Examples

Here are some practical examples of cold storage implementation:

- Personal Cold Storage: An individual might choose a hardware wallet for cold storage. They would set up the wallet, transfer their digital assets to the wallet's address, and then store the device securely. The individual could also back up their wallet's seed phrase on a metal wallet for added security.
- Business Cold Storage: A business holding a substantial amount of digital assets could use a combination of cold storage solutions. It might use a multi-signature hardware wallet for daily transaction needs and store the majority of its assets in a secure cryptocurrency safe or on an air-gapped computer stored in a physical safe.
- Exchange Cold Storage: Cryptocurrency exchanges, which hold substantial amounts of digital assets, typically store the majority of their assets in cold storage to mitigate risk. They use air-gapped computers or hardware security modules stored in secure locations. Multi-signature wallets are often used to require approval from multiple individuals for transactions.

3.6.5 Moving Forward: Cold Storage and Custodial Solutions

With the increasing adoption of digital assets, the demand for secure storage solutions is higher than ever. Cold storage is becoming increasingly sophisticated, with many businesses and individuals turning to digital asset custody services that specialize in secure storage. These services often employ a combination of the cold storage methods outlined above and add additional layers of security, such as physical security measures, multi-signature procedures, and robust backup protocols.

In conclusion, cold storage plays a crucial role in digital asset custody, providing a secure method for storing digital assets offline. By understanding and correctly implementing cold storage, individuals and businesses can significantly enhance the security of their digital assets.

3.7 Hot Wallets and Online Security Measures

While cold storage provides secure offline safeguarding of digital assets, it's not always practical for daily use or for entities that require frequent transactions. That's where hot wallets come in. Hot wallets provide a way to store, manage, and transact digital assets online while implementing robust security measures. This section explores hot wallets, the security measures surrounding their use, and their role in digital asset custody. We'll also delve into practical examples of hot wallet implementations.

3.7.1 Understanding Hot Wallets

A hot wallet is a digital wallet that is connected to the internet. While this connection provides the convenience of easy access and rapid transactions, it also exposes the wallet to potential online threats. Hot wallets can be hosted on a variety of platforms, including desktop computers, mobile devices, and online web services.

3.7.2 The Role of Hot Wallets in Digital Asset Custody

Hot wallets play a crucial role in digital asset custody, particularly for businesses and individuals that need to make frequent transactions. Cryptocurrency exchanges, for example, rely heavily on hot wallets to facilitate instant trades for their users. Similarly, individuals who use digital assets for everyday purchases may find hot wallets more convenient due to their accessibility.

3.7.3 Hot Wallet Security Measures

Given their online exposure, hot wallets require strong security measures to protect against threats. Here are some commonly used security measures:

- Two-Factor Authentication (2FA): This adds an extra layer of security by requiring two forms of authentication before accessing the wallet. Commonly, this is something you know (a password) and something you have (a code sent to a device).
- Multi-Signature Transactions: This requires multiple approvals before a transaction can be completed, providing added security and control.
- Encrypted SSL Connection: This ensures that data transmitted over the internet is encrypted, reducing the risk of interception.
- Regular Software Updates: Keeping the wallet software up to date ensures that the latest security patches are applied.

3.7.4 Types of Hot Wallets

There are several types of hot wallets, each catering to different needs:

- Desktop Wallets: These are software applications installed on a user's personal computer. They provide full control over assets but are only as secure as the computer they're installed on.
- Mobile Wallets: These are apps installed on a smartphone, offering the benefit of making transactions anywhere, including in physical stores through QR code scanning.
- Web Wallets: These are online services that store users' digital assets. They can be accessed from any location and usually offer a user-friendly interface.

- Exchange Wallets: These are provided by digital asset exchanges for users to store, buy, and sell digital assets. While convenient, they're also a popular target for hackers.

3.7.5 Implementing Hot Wallet Solutions: Examples

Let's look at some examples of hot wallet implementation:

- Personal Hot Wallet: An individual might use a desktop wallet for storing digital assets that they frequently transact with. They'd implement security measures such as a strong password, 2FA, and regular software updates.
- Business Hot Wallet: A business might use a multi-signature web wallet for operational needs, requiring approval from multiple departments for each transaction.
- Exchange Hot Wallet: A digital asset exchange would use a series of hot wallets to facilitate user transactions. These would be subject to high-security measures and be supplemented by cold storage for the majority of the assets.

3.7.6 Hot Wallets: Risk and Considerations

While hot wallets offer convenience, they also carry risk due to their constant internet connection. Phishing attempts, malware, and hacking threats are some risks associated with hot wallets. Users must balance the convenience of hot wallets with these risks, and implement proper security measures.

3.7.7 Conclusion: The Balancing Act

Hot wallets are an indispensable component of digital asset custody, primarily due to the convenience and accessibility they offer, attributes that are typically absent in cold storage solutions. Hot wallets enable instantaneous transactions, which are critical for frequent trading, everyday purchases, or any scenario that requires rapid response. Many digital asset exchanges, for example, depend heavily on hot wallets to facilitate real-time trading for their users.

However, with the convenience of hot wallets comes a heightened risk, predominantly due to their constant connection to the internet. This consistent online presence exposes hot wallets to a spectrum of digital threats, including but not limited to, hacking, malware, and phishing attempts. In addition, vulnerabilities in wallet software or the user's device can also be exploited by malicious actors to gain unauthorized access.

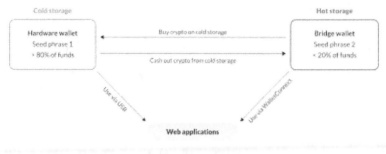

Cold vs hot storage

Consequently, the utilization of hot wallets demands a comprehensive and robust set of security measures. These typically include strong, unique passwords, two-factor authentication (2FA), encrypted SSL connections, and regular software updates. Some wallets also offer multi-signature transactions, which require approval from multiple individuals or devices before a transaction can be completed, adding an extra layer of security.

Even with these measures in place, the inherent risk of hot wallets cannot be entirely eliminated, which brings us to a critical aspect of digital asset custody - balancing security with accessibility. The most common market practice involves using a dual system: hot wallets for operational assets that need to be readily accessible and cold storage for the bulk of assets that aren't required for immediate transactions.

This approach, often referred to as the 'hot/cold wallet strategy,' offers a blend of security and accessibility. Operational assets in the hot wallet are at a higher risk but are readily accessible for quick transactions. At the same time, the majority of assets are safely tucked away in cold storage, completely isolated from online threats. Regular audits and reallocations between the hot wallet and cold storage can ensure that the minimal necessary amount is exposed in the hot wallet, further optimizing the balance.

In conclusion, the key to effective digital asset custody lies in this strategic balancing act, leveraging the strengths of both hot wallets and cold storage solutions. The combination of hot wallets for operational liquidity complemented by the security of cold storage for the majority of assets has proven to be an effective solution in practice, offering both security and accessibility, and is thus widely adopted in the digital asset market.

3.8 Secure Key Management Practices: Protecting Private Keys

In the world of digital assets, private keys are critical. They give users control over their assets and grant them the ability to execute transactions. However, with this power comes significant risk. If private keys fall into the wrong hands, the corresponding assets can be stolen and irretrievably lost. That's why secure key management practices are essential to digital asset custody. In this section, we will explore the importance of private keys, various key management practices, and how they protect digital assets.

3.8.1 Understanding Private Keys

Private keys are long strings of alphanumeric characters that act like the 'password' to a digital asset wallet. They're used to create digital signatures for transactions, which verify the user's ownership of the assets they are sending. Since they provide complete control over one's digital assets, it's imperative that private keys are kept secret and secure.

3.8.2 The Importance of Key Management

Key management refers to the handling and storage of cryptographic keys. It's a critical component of digital asset custody. Proper key management ensures that keys are securely generated, stored, backed up, and retired. A lapse in any of these areas could result in the loss or theft of digital assets.

3.8.3 Key Management Practices

The following are some of the most important key management practices:

- Secure Key Generation: Keys should be generated in a secure environment, using a reputable software or hardware wallet. Some experts recommend generating keys on an air-gapped (offline) computer to ensure they're never exposed to the internet.
- Secure Key Storage: Keys should never be stored in plain text or in easily accessible locations. They should be encrypted and stored in a secure location, such as a hardware wallet or a secure key management system.
- Key Backups: It's essential to have a backup of your private keys in case the original is lost or destroyed. This could be a paper or metal backup stored in a secure location, or a mnemonic seed phrase that can be used to restore the keys.
- Key Rotation: For added security, keys can be periodically changed, or 'rotated'. This requires creating a new key, moving the assets to the new key, and securely deleting the old key.
- Secure Key Retirement: When a key is no longer in use, it should be securely retired. This involves ensuring that all copies of the key are securely deleted and can't be recovered.

3.8.4 Implementing Secure Key Management: Examples

Here are some examples of secure key management implementation:

- Personal Key Management: An individual user might generate a private key using a reputable hardware wallet, write down the backup seed phrase on a piece of paper, and store it in a secure location. They would only enter the private key into their hardware wallet, which remains disconnected from the internet unless a transaction is being made.
- Business Key Management: A business might use a hardware security module (HSM) to generate and store private keys. The HSM would be kept in a secure, monitored location, and the keys would be backed up using a multi-signature scheme, where multiple executives need to provide their signature to access the backup.
- Exchange Key Management: A digital asset exchange would likely use a combination of HSMs and multi-signature wallets to manage keys. The majority of assets would be stored in cold storage, with a smaller amount in a hot wallet for daily transactions. Keys would be rotated regularly, and old keys would be securely retired.

3.8.5 Conclusion: The Role of Secure Key Management in Digital Asset Custody

Secure key management is a critical aspect of digital asset custody. By adhering to best practices in key generation, storage, backup, rotation, and retirement, users can significantly reduce the risk of their digital assets being stolen. The examples provided in this section illustrate how these practices can be implemented in different scenarios, but they should always be adapted to fit individual security needs and risk tolerance.

3.9 Role of Smart Contracts in Digital Asset Custody

Smart contracts represent one of the most powerful applications of blockchain technology. They are self-executing contracts with the terms of the agreement directly written into code. In the context of digital asset custody, smart contracts can add layers of security, automation, and functionality that can greatly enhance the services offered by custodians. This section explores the role of smart contracts in digital asset custody and provides real-world business cases of their implementation.

3.9.1 Understanding Smart Contracts

A smart contract is a program that runs on the blockchain. It's 'smart' because it executes tasks automatically when certain conditions in the code are met. It's a 'contract' because it holds value (in the form of digital assets) and only releases it when the specified conditions are fulfilled. This allows for trustless and automated transactions on the blockchain.

3.9.2 The Role of Smart Contracts in Digital Asset Custody

In the realm of digital asset custody, smart contracts can perform various functions that enhance security and provide additional services:

- Multi-Signature Wallets: Smart contracts can be used to create wallets that require multiple signatures to execute a transaction. This provides an extra layer of security and control over assets.
- Timelocks: Smart contracts can enforce timelocks, which only allow assets to be moved after a certain time or block height. This can protect assets from being quickly moved or stolen.
- Conditional Transactions: Transactions can be programmed to execute only when certain conditions are met, like a particular price level or an external data input.
- Automated Services: Custodians can use smart contracts to offer automated services, such as lending, staking, or yield farming. This can provide additional value to their customers.

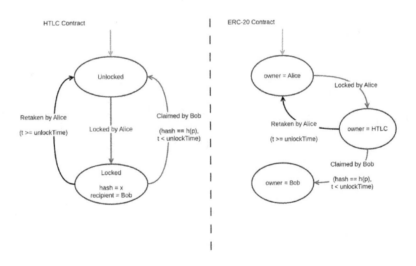

Timelock contract (HTCL)

3.9.3 Implementing Smart Contracts: Business Cases

Let's explore some practical business cases of smart contract implementation in digital asset custody:

- Multi-Signature Wallets for Asset Security: A digital asset custodian could implement a multi-signature smart contract wallet to enhance asset security. For instance, BitGo, a digital asset trust company, uses multi-signature wallets to provide an additional layer of security. Transactions from these wallets require signatures from multiple parties, reducing the risk of asset theft.
- Conditional Transactions for Asset Management: A custodian might use smart contracts to enable conditional transactions. For instance, a smart contract could be set up to automatically move a customer's assets into a different cryptocurrency if the price of the current one drops to a certain level.
- Automated Yield Farming: A custodian could use smart contracts to provide automated yield farming services. This could involve automatically investing a customer's assets in various DeFi protocols to maximize returns. For example, Yearn.Finance employs smart contracts to automatically switch users' funds between different DeFi lending protocols to chase the best yield.
- Staking-as-a-Service: A custodian could use smart contracts to provide staking services. Customers could stake their proof-of-stake cryptocurrencies directly from their custody account, earning staking rewards without managing the staking process themselves. An example here is Coinbase Custody, which provides staking services for various cryptocurrencies.

3.9.4 Conclusion: Smart Contracts Enhancing Digital Asset Custody

Smart contracts are changing the way we interact with digital assets, adding layers of automation, functionality, and security. Their role in digital asset custody is growing, as they enable custodians to enhance their security measures and offer innovative services that provide added value to their customers. The practical examples provided in this section illustrate the transformative potential of smart contracts in

3.10 Interoperability and Cross-Chain Solutions

One of the central challenges in the blockchain space is interoperability, or the ability for different blockchains to communicate and interact with each other. In the context of digital asset custody, this becomes especially important as custodians need to manage assets across a variety of blockchains. This section will explore the concept of interoperability, its importance in digital asset custody, and the role of cross-chain solutions.

3.10.1 Understanding Interoperability

Interoperability in the blockchain context refers to the ability of different blockchain systems to exchange and make use of information. Just as the internet connected isolated computers into a global network, blockchain interoperability seeks to connect isolated blockchains into a global blockchain network.

3.10.2 The Importance of Interoperability in Digital Asset Custody

Digital asset custodians manage a wide range of assets, each of which may reside on a different blockchain. Bitcoin resides on the Bitcoin blockchain, Ether on the Ethereum blockchain, and so on. Without interoperability, these assets are siloed on their respective blockchains, limiting the ability of custodians to manage them in a unified manner.

Interoperability provides the ability for custodians to manage assets across multiple blockchains in a seamless manner. It can enable the transfer of assets between different blockchains, allow for cross-chain transactions, and even enable complex interactions between smart contracts on different blockchains.

3.10.3 Cross-Chain Solutions: Bridging the Blockchain Divide

Several solutions have been proposed and developed to address the issue of blockchain interoperability. These are often referred to as cross-chain solutions. While the specifics of these solutions can vary, they generally work by creating a sort of 'bridge' between blockchains that allows for the transfer of information and assets.

Here are a few prominent cross-chain solutions:

- Polkadot: Polkadot allows different blockchains to interoperate while maintaining their own unique consensus and governance models. It achieves this through a central relay chain and various parachains (individual blockchains) that connect to it.
- Cosmos: Like Polkadot, Cosmos is a network of interconnected blockchains. Cosmos uses a different approach, with a central hub and various zones (individual blockchains) that connect to it.
- Wrapped Assets: Wrapped assets are tokenized representations of a digital asset from one blockchain on another blockchain. For example, Wrapped Bitcoin (WBTC) is a token on the Ethereum blockchain that represents an actual Bitcoin.

3.10.4 Implementing Interoperability in Digital Asset Custody

Here's how digital asset custodians might implement interoperability:

- Cross-Chain Asset Management: Custodians can use cross-chain solutions to manage assets across multiple blockchains in a unified manner. For instance, a custodian might use Polkadot to manage assets on both the Ethereum and Bitcoin blockchains.
- Cross-Chain Services: Custodians can offer services that take advantage of cross-chain functionality. For example, a custodian might offer a service that allows customers to easily move assets between different blockchains.
- Wrapped Assets: Custodians can support wrapped assets, allowing customers to use their assets on different blockchains. For instance, a custodian might allow a customer to deposit Bitcoin and then use Wrapped Bitcoin in Ethereum-based decentralized finance (DeFi) protocols.

3.10.5 Conclusion: Interoperability Enhancing Digital Asset Custody

Interoperability is key to unlocking the full potential of the blockchain space, and its importance in digital asset custody cannot be overstated. As cross-chain solutions continue to develop and mature, the ability to seamlessly manage and interact with assets across multiple blockchains will become a standard feature of digital asset custody. The examples provided in this section illustrate how interoperability is already beginning to shape the future of digital asset custody.

3.11 Privacy and Anonymity Considerations in Custodial Technology

In a world that is increasingly connected, privacy and anonymity have become crucial. Digital asset custody, by its very nature, involves the storage and management of assets that are not only financially valuable, but also information-rich. In this regard, privacy and anonymity considerations are not just optional, but integral to a custodian's operations. This section delves into the nuances of privacy and anonymity in the realm of custodial technology, its importance, challenges, and the methods being adopted to tackle them.

3.11.1 Privacy & Anonymity: What Does It Mean?

In the realm of digital asset custody, privacy typically refers to the ability of an individual or an organization to withhold their information from being disclosed without their consent. This includes personal information, financial data, transaction details, and more. Anonymity, on the other hand, is the ability of individuals or organizations to perform actions (such as transactions) without revealing their identity.

3.11.2 The Imperative of Privacy and Anonymity in Custodial Services

Why does privacy matter in digital asset custody? The answer lies in the fact that any breach of privacy can lead to a multitude of problems - from identity theft and financial loss to potential legal issues.

Anonymity, on the other hand, can play a crucial role in protecting the identity of the owner of the assets. While blockchains are transparent, the pseudonymous nature of blockchain transactions can still allow users to keep their identities hidden if properly handled.

3.11.3 The Challenges of Upholding Privacy & Anonymity

Maintaining privacy and anonymity in digital asset custody is a task laden with challenges. While blockchain technology offers significant advantages in terms of security, the decentralized and transparent nature of public blockchains can potentially jeopardize privacy. Every transaction is recorded on a public ledger, visible to anyone who wishes to inspect it.

Similarly, while anonymity is one of the cornerstones of many cryptocurrencies, in practice, achieving true anonymity is a complex task due to regulatory requirements, such as Anti-Money Laundering (AML) and Know Your Customer (KYC) regulations.

3.11.4 Addressing Privacy & Anonymity: Strategies and Technologies

Various strategies and technologies can be employed to uphold privacy and anonymity in digital asset custody. These include:

- Using Privacy Coins: Privacy coins like Monero or ZCash are designed to provide greater privacy and anonymity. They use techniques such as ring signatures or zk-SNARKs to obfuscate the transaction details.
- Layer-2 Solutions: Layer-2 solutions like the Lightning Network for Bitcoin or Plasma for Ethereum can potentially increase privacy as they allow transactions to occur off-chain, away from the public eye.
- Mixing Services: These services mix potentially identifiable or 'tainted' cryptocurrency funds with others, making it hard to track them back to the source.
- Zero-Knowledge Proofs: This is a method by which one party can prove to another that a given statement is true, without conveying any additional information. This has huge potential for maintaining privacy in blockchain transactions.

3.11.5 Use Case: Privacy and Anonymity in Digital Asset Custody

An example of privacy and anonymity considerations in custodial technology can be seen in the operation of custodial wallets. These wallets not only have to maintain the security of the private keys, but they also have to ensure that the transaction data, personal information, and other sensitive data remain confidential.

The use of secure hardware, encrypted connections, and secure protocols is standard. Beyond that, certain custodians might provide the option to use privacy-enhancing technologies or services, depending on the risk appetite and preference of the customer.

In conclusion, privacy and anonymity are essential considerations in digital asset custody. As regulations evolve and privacy-preserving technologies mature, it will be important for custodians to strike a balance between maintaining privacy and compliance with legal requirements.

4 Designing a Secure Custodial Infrastructure

4.1 Understanding the Security Imperatives in Digital Asset Custody

In the realm of digital asset custody, security is paramount. The ability to protect digital assets from theft, loss, and other forms of compromise is the cornerstone of a custodian's value proposition. But understanding the full breadth and depth of the security imperative requires us to first comprehend the unique challenges posed by digital assets, the stakes involved, and the landscape of threats that custodians must navigate.

4.1.1 Defining the Security Imperative

At its core, the security imperative in digital asset custody is about safeguarding the integrity of digital assets, ensuring that they are always available to their rightful owners and that unauthorized parties can't access them. In contrast to traditional assets, digital assets exist purely in the digital realm, which brings unique challenges.

4.1.2 Unique Challenges of Digital Asset Security

Digital assets, due to their inherent nature, have unique security vulnerabilities. For instance, if private keys associated with a digital wallet are lost, the assets within are irretrievable. If they're stolen, there's rarely any recourse. These risks are exacerbated by the borderless, 24/7 nature of the digital asset markets, which leaves little room for downtime and makes digital assets a lucrative target for cybercriminals worldwide.

4.1.3 The High Stakes of Digital Asset Custody

The stakes in digital asset custody are exceptionally high. A security breach could result in significant financial losses and severe reputational damage that could threaten the custodian's very existence. This situation is intensified by the relatively unregulated nature of the digital asset market and the pace at which it's evolving.

4.1.4 The Threat Landscape

The threat landscape that custodians must navigate is vast and varied. It includes external threats from hackers who are constantly evolving their tactics, techniques, and procedures. Internal threats can come from employees, whether through negligence, insider threats, or the potential for collusion with external parties. Additionally, systemic threats can arise from vulnerabilities in the underlying blockchain technology, dependence on third-party technologies, and more.

4.1.5 Regulatory and Legal Considerations

Regulation and legal considerations also play a critical role in the security imperative. With the rapidly evolving landscape of digital asset regulations across different jurisdictions, custodians need to ensure they're compliant with applicable laws and regulations. This can involve measures such as Know Your Customer (KYC) and Anti-Money Laundering (AML) procedures, reporting, and record-keeping requirements.

4.1.6 The Role of Technology

Technological solutions form the bedrock of security in digital asset custody. This includes technologies for secure storage of private keys, secure transaction processing, intrusion detection and prevention, identity and access management, data protection, and more. But while technology is part of the solution, it's not a silver bullet – effective security also requires robust operational processes, organizational policies, and a culture of security.

4.1.7 Building Trust

Ultimately, the security imperative is also about building trust. In a market characterized by high levels of uncertainty and risk, being able to demonstrate robust security can help custodians win the trust of their clients. This involves transparency in security practices, independent audits, and certifications, as well as clear and prompt communication in case of security incidents.

In conclusion, understanding the security imperatives in digital asset custody is about acknowledging the unique challenges, high stakes, and the vast and varied threat landscape. It's about leveraging technology while understanding its limits and focusing on building trust with clients. In the following sections, we will delve deeper into each of these topics, providing you with the knowledge you need to design and implement a secure custodial infrastructure.

5 Advanced Security Measures in Digital Asset Custody

As the world of digital assets continues to evolve, so too does the threat landscape surrounding it. To stay ahead of potential threats, the world of digital asset custody must constantly adapt and innovate. One arena where this innovation is most pronounced is in the use of cryptographic techniques. In this section, we dive deep into the pioneering cryptographic methods that are reshaping how assets are secured in the digital domain.

5. 1 Security Measures in Digital Asset Custody

5.1.1 Understanding Cryptography's Role

Before delving into the advanced techniques, it's essential to understand the foundational role cryptography plays in digital asset custody. At its essence, cryptography provides two main functions: confidentiality and authenticity. Through various algorithms and techniques, cryptography ensures that data remains confidential and that the sender of the data can be authenticated.

5.1.2 Traditional Cryptographic Techniques

Traditionally, digital asset security has revolved around public and private key encryption. Using asymmetric cryptography, digital assets can be secured using a private key, while transactions and interactions can be verified using a corresponding public key. Techniques such as the Elliptic Curve Digital Signature Algorithm (ECDSA) have been central to many blockchain and digital asset technologies.

5.1.3 Threshold Signatures: Beyond Traditional Key Management

One of the groundbreaking cryptographic methods is threshold signatures. Unlike traditional methods where a single private key signs a transaction, threshold signatures split the key into multiple shares. A predetermined number of these shares are then required to produce a signature. This method dramatically enhances security by ensuring that even if some key shares are compromised, transactions remain secure unless a threshold is reached.

5.1.4 Homomorphic Encryption: Computation on Ciphertexts

Homomorphic encryption allows for computations to be performed on encrypted data without first decrypting it. In the context of digital asset custody, this means that certain operations, like balance checks or transaction validations, can be performed without exposing the raw data, offering an added layer of security against both internal and external threats.

5.1.5 zk-SNARKs and Zero-Knowledge Proofs

Zero-knowledge proofs, particularly zk-SNARKs (Zero-Knowledge Succinct Non-Interactive Argument of Knowledge), are cryptographic methods allowing one party to prove they know a value without revealing that value. In digital asset custody, this can ensure privacy and confidentiality in transactions, allowing for verification without exposing critical transaction details.

In the field of information security, the term "zero-knowledge" is often used to describe a well-designed security architecture that applies the need-to-know principle to IT components. However, in cryptography research, zero-knowledge has a more precise definition.

A zero-knowledge proof is a cryptographic protocol that allows one party (the prover) to convince another party (the verifier) that they know the solution to a mathematical problem without revealing the solution itself. The Schnorr protocol is a popular example that enables a prover to prove they know $x=\log_g y$ to a verifier who knows y and g.

Zero-knowledge proofs for simple equations are relatively easy and efficient. However, the challenge for cryptographers in recent years has been to make these proofs work efficiently for more complex and arbitrary operations.

The first breakthrough was achieved with token transactions, as demonstrated by the Zcash protocol. Proofs were created to verify that a coin not previously spent was sent from one user to another, their hidden balances were adjusted accordingly, and the first user could not send the coin again.

Extending zero-knowledge proofs to arbitrary operations was initially thought to be impossible. However, researchers have made significant progress in recent years, culminating in techniques such as ZEXE.

Zero-knowledge based applications offer numerous benefits, including scalability and reduced resource consumption for verifying blockchain operations. Private computation is particularly useful in digital finance for protecting client identifiable information, financial balances, and metadata while enabling regulatory compliance and supporting more complex on-chain operations at a reasonable cost.

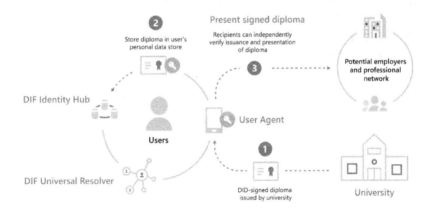

Microsoft Tech: Advancing Privacy with Zero-Knowledge Proof Credentials

5.1.6 Post-Quantum Cryptography: Preparing for Tomorrow

The emerging field of quantum computing poses a potential threat to classical encryption techniques. As such, the development of post-quantum cryptographic methods, resistant to quantum attacks, has become essential. Techniques such as lattice-based cryptography, hash-based cryptography, and multivariate polynomial cryptography are under intense research and development to ensure the future-proofing of digital asset security.

5.1.7 Real-World Implementation and Challenges

Implementing these pioneering cryptographic techniques is not without challenges. The real-world application requires considerations of computational overhead, integration with existing systems, and potential vulnerabilities specific to each method. Additionally, as the regulatory landscape around digital assets continues to develop, ensuring compliance while leveraging advanced cryptographic techniques poses its set of challenges.

5.1.8 Conclusion: The Road Ahead in Cryptographic Innovation

The arena of cryptography in digital asset custody is dynamic and continually evolving. With the ever-increasing value and adoption of digital assets, the stakes have never been higher. As custodians and technology providers continue to innovate, staying informed and educated about these pioneering cryptographic techniques will be paramount for anyone involved in the industry.

In the sections to follow, we will delve deeper into each of these cutting-edge techniques, providing in-depth insights, case studies, and best practices in their implementation and management.

5.2 Quantum-Resistant Protocols: Preparing for the Future

In the realm of cryptography and digital asset security, one looming specter stands poised to disrupt all we know about encryption and protection: quantum computing. While its full-scale application remains on the horizon, its theoretical implications for cryptographic algorithms are profound. Current cryptographic standards, which ensure the security of our digital assets, may be rendered obsolete. Therefore, the development and understanding of quantum-resistant protocols are crucial. In this section, we'll explore the quantum threat, its implications for digital asset custody, and the strategies being developed to counteract it.

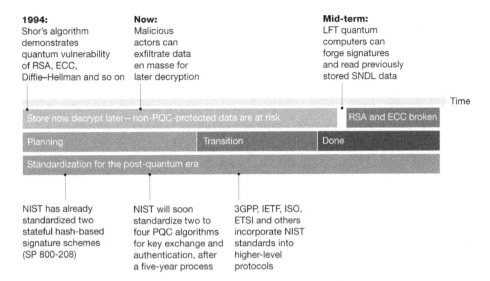

Nature: Transitioning organizations to post-quantum cryptography

5.2.1 Grasping the Quantum Threat

Before we dive into the protocols, it's imperative to understand the threat quantum computing poses to cryptography. Unlike classical computers, which use bits (0s or 1s), quantum computers use quantum bits, or qubits. These qubits, through the phenomena of superposition and entanglement, enable quantum computers to solve certain problems exponentially faster than their classical counterparts.

For cryptography, this speed poses a problem. Algorithms such as RSA or ECC, which rely on the difficulty of factoring large numbers or computing discrete logarithms, could be broken in moments by a sufficiently powerful quantum computer.

5.2.2 Quantum Computing Vs. Today's Cryptography

Many cryptographic processes today are secure because they rely on problems that are computationally hard for classical computers. But with Shor's algorithm, a quantum computer could factor large numbers or compute discrete logarithms in polynomial time, rendering widely-used encryption methods like RSA or ECC insecure.

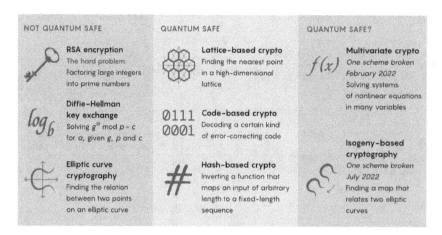

Types of cryptographic

5.2.3 Towards Quantum-Resistant Cryptography

Quantum-resistant or post-quantum cryptographic algorithms are being designed to secure data even in the face of a quantum computing threat. These are not based on quantum mechanics but are cryptographic methods believed to be secure against quantum attacks.

5.2.4 Popular Quantum-Resistant Algorithms

- Lattice-based cryptography: This approach relies on the hardness of certain problems in lattice theory. Algorithms like Learning With Errors (LWE) or Ring-LWE are considered strong contenders for post-quantum cryptography.
- Hash-based cryptography: Widely regarded as the most mature form of post-quantum cryptography, it involves creating digital signatures using hash functions. The Merkle signature scheme, for example, has been around since the late 1970s and is believed to be quantum-resistant.
- Code-based cryptography: Relying on the hardness of decoding randomly generated linear codes, the McEliece cryptosystem is a key example and has resisted cryptanalysis since its introduction in 1978.
- Multivariate polynomial cryptography: Based on the problem of finding solutions to systems of multivariate polynomials, this method has shown promise, but challenges related to key sizes and efficiency remain.

5.2.5 Practical Implementation and Challenges

While the theories underpinning quantum-resistant algorithms are solid, their practical application in the real world, particularly in digital asset custody, presents challenges:

- Performance: Quantum-resistant algorithms often require more computational power or have larger key sizes, which can be an issue for real-world systems and networks.

- Interoperability: Ensuring that quantum-resistant algorithms can work seamlessly with existing infrastructure is crucial.
- Continuous evolution: The world of quantum research is dynamic. As quantum computers become more powerful, the cryptographic community must be ready to adapt and evolve.

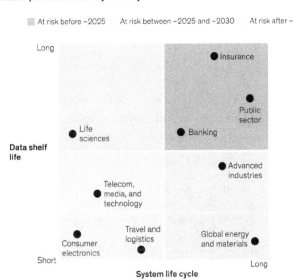

Risk of quantum-powered attack by industry

5.2.6 Case Study: Quantum-Resistant Blockchain

Several blockchain projects are exploring quantum-resistant methods. One notable example is the QRL (Quantum Resistant Ledger) project, which claims to be fully resistant to quantum attacks using a hash-based signature scheme.

5.2.7 Conclusion: The Path Forward in Quantum Security

While quantum computers capable of breaking current cryptographic standards aren't yet a reality, the clock is ticking. It is a race to ensure that by the time such quantum computers exist, our digital asset infrastructures are already well-shielded. As with all things in cybersecurity, the key is to be proactive rather than reactive.

5.3 AI and Machine Learning: Predictive Threat Analysis

The world of digital assets, teeming with rapid transactions and vast datasets, presents unique challenges. In such an environment, traditional methods of threat detection might not suffice. Enter Artificial Intelligence (AI) and Machine Learning (ML) - cutting-edge technologies that promise to revolutionize how we approach security in digital asset custody. This section delves into the integration of AI and ML in predictive threat analysis, offering insights into the promise and perils of these technologies.

5.3.1 An Overview: AI & ML in Cybersecurity

AI and ML are subsets of computer science where systems are designed to perform tasks that traditionally required human intelligence. In cybersecurity, this means detecting threats, analyzing patterns, and even predicting future vulnerabilities. The immense volume of data within digital asset systems makes them a prime candidate for AI and ML integration.

5.3.2 The Need for Predictive Threat Analysis

Traditional security mechanisms often work on set rules or signatures. They react to known threats. However, the evolving landscape of cyber-attacks requires a more proactive approach. Predictive threat analysis aims to anticipate threats before they materialize, providing an early warning system of sorts.

5.3.3 How Machine Learning Powers Predictive Analysis

At the heart of predictive threat analysis lies Machine Learning. Here's how it works:

- Data Ingestion: ML algorithms require data to train on. This data often comes from logs, transactions, and other system activities.
- Feature Extraction: Important characteristics, or features, are extracted from this data. For digital assets, this might include transaction size, frequency, or originating IP addresses.
- Model Training: Using historical data, the algorithm is trained to recognize patterns associated with malicious activities.
- Real-time Analysis: Once trained, the model analyzes real-time data, identifying anomalies or patterns that might suggest a potential threat.

5.3.4 AI in Anomaly Detection

While ML is exceptional at pattern recognition, AI takes things a step further. AI systems can make decisions based on the data. In the context of digital asset custody, this means automatically flagging suspicious transactions, temporarily halting potentially malicious activities, or even dynamically adjusting security protocols in response to perceived threats.

5.3.5 Real-world Implementations

Several digital asset custodians are already leveraging AI and ML. For example:

- Automated Threat Intelligence: Platforms that use AI to trawl the dark web, hacker forums, and other sources, looking for potential threats or mentions of vulnerabilities.
- Behavioral Analysis: Systems that learn the 'normal' behavior of users or network traffic and alert administrators to anomalies that might suggest a breach or attack.

5.3.6 The Challenges and Ethical Considerations

Relying on AI and ML isn't without its challenges:

- Data Quality: ML models are only as good as the data they're trained on. Inaccurate or biased data can lead to false positives or overlooked threats.
- Over-reliance: While AI can enhance security, over-reliance can be dangerous. Human oversight remains essential.
- Ethical Concerns: AI systems might infringe on privacy, especially when analyzing user behaviors or personal transactions.

5.3.7 Preparing for the AI-powered Security Era

Embracing AI and ML in digital asset custody requires preparation:

- Infrastructure Investment: Powerful computing resources are needed to process vast amounts of data in real-time.
- Training & Education: Security personnel need to be trained to work alongside AI, understanding its strengths and limitations.
- Regulatory Compliance: As with all things in digital asset custody, ensuring AI and ML tools comply with existing and emerging regulations is paramount.

5.3.8 Conclusion: A Paradigm Shift in Digital Asset Security

AI and ML represent a seismic shift in how we approach security in the digital realm. While challenges exist, the potential benefits - especially in predictive threat analysis - are too significant to ignore. As these technologies mature and integrate deeper into the world of digital asset custody, they promise a future where threats are anticipated, addressed, and neutralized with unprecedented precision.

5.4 Biometric Security: Beyond Passwords and Keys

In the evolving landscape of digital asset custody, one of the most innovative yet personal layers of security being integrated is biometric authentication. Where passwords can be forgotten and cryptographic keys can be lost or stolen, biometrics offers a form of verification that's unique to each individual: their very own biological or behavioral traits. From the intricacies of a retina scan to the rhythm of a person's keystrokes, biometric security is redefining how we think about access and identity in the digital space. This section delves deep into the world of biometrics, its implications for digital asset custody, and the advantages and challenges of its implementation.

5.4.1 Biometrics: An Introduction

Biometrics refers to the measurement and statistical analysis of people's unique physical and behavioral characteristics. The term itself derives from the Greek words "bio" (life) and "metric" (to measure). Used for identification and access control, biometrics can be a standalone security measure or combined with other methods for multi-factor authentication.

5.4.2 The Spectrum of Biometric Modalities

Biometric systems utilize various modalities, each offering its unique advantages:

- Fingerprint Recognition: One of the most widespread forms, it uses the unique patterns of ridges and valleys on a fingertip.
- Facial Recognition: Harnesses distinct facial features and contours to identify individuals.
- Iris and Retina Scanning: Focuses on the unique patterns found within the eye.
- Voice Recognition: Uses the distinct sound and pattern of an individual's voice.
- Behavioral Biometrics: Less about physical traits and more about patterns of behavior, like typing rhythms or device-handling habits.

5.4.3 Integration into Digital Asset Custody

In the domain of digital assets, ensuring the right person accesses the right assets is paramount. Here's how biometrics is enhancing the security matrix:

- Access Control: Biometrics ensures that only authorized individuals can access digital wallets or transaction portals.
- Transaction Verification: For high-value transactions, biometrics can serve as an additional verification layer.
- Audit Trails: Biometric logs offer irrefutable records of who accessed what and when, crucial for compliance and forensic analysis.

5.4.4 Advantages of Biometric Systems

- Uniqueness: Every individual's biometric data is inherently unique.
- Difficult to Forge: Replicating or faking biometric data is challenging compared to passwords or tokens.
- Convenience: No need to remember passwords or carry physical tokens.
- Integrated Multi-factor Authentication: Biometrics can be part of a comprehensive MFA strategy.

5.4.5 The Challenges in Biometric Implementation

- Data Sensitivity: Biometric data, once compromised, can't be reset like a password.

74

- Storage and Privacy Concerns: How and where biometric data is stored raises concerns, especially with regulations like GDPR or CCPA.
- False Positives/Negatives: No system is foolproof; biometrics too can occasionally misidentify or fail to recognize.

5.4.6 Biometrics in a Decentralized World

One exciting frontier is the integration of biometrics in decentralized systems like blockchains. Projects are exploring how biometric data can be stored and accessed on decentralized ledgers while maintaining user privacy.

5.4.7 Ethical and Privacy Implications

The integration of biometrics into any system, especially something as personal as digital asset custody, comes with ethical implications:

- Informed Consent: Users must be fully aware of how their data will be used.
- Data Storage: Ensuring data isn't susceptible to breaches.
- Potential Misuse: Concerns about data being used for other purposes, like surveillance.

5.4.8 Future of Biometrics in Digital Custody

Emerging technologies promise even more advanced biometric solutions:

- Gait Analysis: Identifying people by how they walk.
- Heartbeat Identification: Using one's unique cardiac rhythm.
- Brainwave Patterns: Potentially the most unique biometric of all, but still in nascent stages.

5.4.9 Conclusion: A Personal Touch to Digital Security

As the world of digital asset custody evolves, ensuring a harmonious blend of security and user experience is crucial. Biometrics stands at the forefront of this evolution, offering a unique blend of the two. While challenges remain, the future promises even more advanced and personal ways to secure our digital treasures.

5.5 Deep Cold Storage: The Fort Knox of Digital Assets

As the importance and value of digital assets grow, so does the need for ensuring their utmost security. Traditional cold storage methods, while effective, have seen innovations pushing them even further into zones of absolute security. Deep cold storage represents the pinnacle of these efforts, acting as the Fort Knox for digital assets. In this section, we will embark on a journey deep into the recesses of this security paradigm, exploring its foundations, methods, benefits, and potential drawbacks.

5.5.1 The Evolution of Digital Asset Storage

To appreciate deep cold storage, one must first understand the journey of digital asset storage:

- Hot Wallets: Constantly connected to the internet, ideal for frequent transactions but vulnerable to online threats.
- Cold Storage: Offline storage methods, greatly reducing exposure to online attacks.
- Deep Cold Storage: An enhanced form of cold storage, emphasizing multiple layers of offline protection.

5.5.2 Understanding Deep Cold Storage

Deep cold storage can be likened to a vault within a vault. It's not merely about being offline; it's about adding extra layers of physical and digital protection to ensure assets remain beyond the reach of malevolent actors.

5.5.3 Key Characteristics of Deep Cold Storage

- Air-Gapped Systems: Computers used to access deep cold storage are never connected to public networks.
- Physical Barriers: Stored in locations with multiple security barriers, often undisclosed or underground.
- Multi-Signature Protocols: Requires multiple authentication steps, often involving different individuals, to access the assets.
- Regular Audits: Even though assets are offline, regular audits are conducted to ensure their integrity.

5.5.4 Constructing a Deep Cold Storage System

- Selecting Hardware: Dedicated, uncompromised hardware is essential. This often means purchasing new devices solely for storage purposes.
- Setting Up the Environment: Ensure the storage environment is free from electronic interference and is physically secure.
- Data Transfer: Transfer of data to deep cold storage devices must be done securely, often via one-time-use devices.
- Auditing & Maintenance: Regular checks to ensure the integrity of the storage system and updates to the security protocol as needed.

5.5.5 Benefits of Deep Cold Storage

- Enhanced Security: By virtue of being offline and behind multiple security barriers, the risk of theft is minimal.
- Protection from Digital Threats: Immune to malware, ransomware, and other forms of digital attacks.

- Peace of Mind: For investors and institutions, knowing assets are in deep cold storage can be reassuring.

5.5.6 Potential Drawbacks and Challenges

- Liquidity Issues: Accessing assets can be time-consuming, which can be problematic for those requiring quick liquidity.
- Costly Implementation: Setting up a secure environment, purchasing dedicated hardware, and routine audits can be expensive.
- Operational Challenges: Requires a strict protocol for accessing assets, which can be operationally cumbersome.

5.5.7 The Future: Is There Anything Deeper Than Deep Cold Storage?

As with all tech domains, innovation never stops. Concepts such as quantum encryption and decentralized storage across distributed ledgers (ensuring no single point of failure) are on the horizon, promising even greater security enhancements.

5.5.8 Conclusion: The Zenith of Digital Asset Protection

Deep cold storage, while not without its challenges, represents the zenith in digital asset protection currently available. As the digital realm continues to grow and evolve, so will the methods we employ to safeguard its treasures. The Fort Knox of today might well be the foundation for the citadels of tomorrow.

5.6 Blockchain Forensics and Anomaly Detection

In the ever-evolving domain of digital asset custody, one field rapidly gaining traction is blockchain forensics. As digital asset transactions become increasingly complex and the volume on blockchains grows exponentially, the need for sophisticated tools to analyze, track, and highlight anomalous activity becomes imperative. This section shines a light on the world of blockchain forensics, unraveling the nuances of anomaly detection, its importance, methodologies, and the challenges it seeks to address.

5.6.1 What is Blockchain Forensics?

At its core, blockchain forensics revolves around analyzing blockchain data to extract meaningful patterns, insights, and intelligence. It's a science and an art, leveraging technology to decode the vast, decentralized ledgers that underpin digital assets.

5.6.2 The Genesis: Why Do We Need Blockchain Forensics?

As decentralized systems, blockchains offer transparency but can also be labyrinthine. The public nature of transactions does not always translate to traceability or comprehensibility. Forensics steps in to:

- Identify illicit activities or funds.
- Track funds across multiple transactions.
- Provide evidence for legal or compliance proceedings.

5.6.3 Anomaly Detection: The Heart of Forensics

Anomalies refer to patterns or activities that deviate from the norm. In blockchain:

- Unusually large transactions.
- Rapid sequences of transactions.
- Transactions to or from blacklisted addresses.

Detecting these anomalies in real-time is vital to prevent potential misuse or illicit activities.

5.6.4 Tools and Techniques

Forensic specialists employ a range of sophisticated tools:

- Pattern Recognition Algorithms: To identify repeated sequences or suspicious activities.
- Heuristics Analysis: Useful for identifying suspicious wallet addresses or activity clusters.
- Graph Analysis: Given the interconnected nature of blockchains, graph techniques can unravel transaction chains.

5.6.5 Real-world Implementations

Companies like Chainalysis and Elliptic specialize in blockchain forensics, offering tools and services that:

- Track stolen funds.
- Identify wallets associated with illicit activities.
- Aid law enforcement in digital investigations.

5.6.6 Challenges in Blockchain Forensics

Despite advances, several challenges persist:

- Privacy Coins: Currencies like Monero and Zcash emphasize transactional privacy, complicating forensic efforts.
- Off-chain Transactions: Not all digital asset transfers occur on public blockchains.
- Mixers and Tumblers: Services that jumble transactions to obfuscate the origins and destinations.

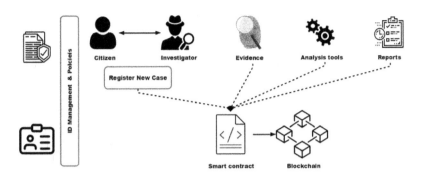

Forensic flow and blockchain integration

5.6.7 Ethical and Privacy Concerns

Forensics, while crucial, raises concerns:

- Surveillance Risks: Tools could be misused for broader surveillance agendas.
- Privacy Invasion: Overreaching forensic tools might intrude on users' financial privacy.

5.6.8 The Road Ahead: Future of Blockchain Forensics

Emerging technologies promise even deeper insights:

- Integration with AI: To predict and preemptively detect illicit activities.
- Cross-chain Analysis: As assets move across blockchains, forensics will need to keep pace.

5.6.9 Conclusion: Balancing Security and Privacy

Blockchain forensics embodies the tension between transparency and privacy. As the tools and techniques of this field become more advanced, the broader crypto community will need to engage in continuous dialogue to ensure a balance between security, transparency, and individual privacy.

5.7 Decentralized Custody Solutions: A New Paradigm

In the rapidly evolving digital asset ecosystem, the concept of custody has taken on a new dimension. Traditional financial institutions have long relied on centralized custodians to safeguard their clients' assets, but the emergence of cryptocurrencies and other digital assets has introduced a new set of challenges and opportunities. In this section, we will explore the rise of decentralized custody solutions, their unique characteristics, and the potential they hold for reshaping the digital asset landscape.

5.7.1 The Need for Decentralized Custody

The primary function of a custodian is to securely hold and manage assets on behalf of clients. In the traditional financial world, this role is typically performed by banks or other regulated institutions, which are entrusted with safeguarding assets such as cash, securities, and real estate.

However, the advent of cryptocurrencies like Bitcoin has disrupted this traditional model. Unlike traditional assets, cryptocurrencies are digital in nature and rely on cryptographic keys for access and control. This means that the security of these assets is fundamentally different from that of physical or paper-based assets.

Centralized custody solutions have emerged to address these challenges, but they come with their own set of issues. First and foremost, they introduce a single point of failure: if the centralized custodian is compromised, the assets under its control are at risk. Additionally, centralized custodians can be subject to regulatory scrutiny and may be required to comply with strict rules and regulations that may not align with the ethos of decentralized finance (DeFi).

Decentralized custody solutions offer an alternative to this centralized model, providing a more resilient and secure way to store and manage digital assets. By leveraging blockchain technology and smart contracts, these solutions can eliminate the need for trusted intermediaries and enable users to maintain direct control over their assets.

5.7.2 Characteristics of Decentralized Custody Solutions

Decentralized custody solutions possess several key characteristics that set them apart from their centralized counterparts. These include:

- Non-custodial control: Unlike centralized custody solutions, which require users to relinquish control of their assets to a third party, decentralized custody solutions enable users to maintain direct control over their assets. This is typically achieved through the use of cryptographic keys or other forms of access control that are held by the user, rather than the custodian.
- Decentralized security: Decentralized custody solutions leverage blockchain technology to create a distributed network of nodes that collectively secure the assets under management. This eliminates the single point of failure inherent in centralized systems and provides a higher level of security against hacks, fraud, and other forms of compromise.
- Programmability: Many decentralized custody solutions are built on top of programmable blockchains like Ethereum, which allows them to incorporate complex logic and functionality through the use of smart contracts. This can enable features such as automated asset management, multi-signature access control, and customizable security protocols.
- Transparency: Decentralized custody solutions often provide greater transparency than their centralized counterparts, as transactions and asset holdings can be publicly verified on the blockchain. This can help to build trust among users and reduce the risk of fraud or mismanagement.
- Regulatory considerations: Decentralized custody solutions may not be subject to the same regulatory requirements as traditional custodians, as they do not involve the transfer of control or ownership of assets to a third party. However, this is an evolving area of regulation, and the legal status of decentralized custody solutions may vary depending on the jurisdiction and specific implementation.

5.7.3 Key Components of Decentralized Custody Solutions

There are several core components that underpin decentralized custody solutions, including:

- Blockchain technology: The foundation of decentralized custody solutions is blockchain technology, which provides a secure, distributed ledger for recording transactions and asset holdings. By leveraging the inherent security and transparency of blockchains, decentralized custody solutions can provide a more resilient and trustless alternative to centralized systems.
- Smart contracts: Many decentralized custody solutions rely on smart contracts to automate key functions and enforce security protocols. Smart contracts are self-executing pieces of code that run on a blockchain, and they can be used to implement features such as multi-signature access control, time-locked withdrawals, and automated asset management.
- Cryptographic keys: Decentralized custody solutions use cryptographic keys to secure access to assets and enable users to maintain direct control over their holdings. These keys are typically generated and stored on the user's device or in a hardware wallet, ensuring that they remain in the user's possession at all times.
- Multi-signature schemes: Some decentralized custody solutions employ multi-signature schemes to enhance security and provide additional layers of access control. In a multi-signature setup, multiple keys are required to authorize a transaction or perform other sensitive actions, which can help protect against theft or unauthorized access.
- Interoperability: Decentralized custody solutions often prioritize interoperability with other blockchain networks and digital asset ecosystems. This can enable users to seamlessly manage a diverse range of assets across multiple platforms and benefit from the growing ecosystem of DeFi services and applications.

5.7.4 Decentralized Custody Solution Use Cases

Decentralized custody solutions have a wide range of potential use cases within the digital asset ecosystem, including:

- Individual asset management: Decentralized custody solutions can provide individuals with a secure and convenient way to manage their digital assets without relying on centralized intermediaries. This can empower users to take greater control over their financial lives and benefit from the growing range of DeFi services and applications.
- Institutional asset management: As institutional interest in digital assets continues to grow, decentralized custody solutions can offer a more secure and flexible alternative to traditional custodial services. By leveraging the unique characteristics of decentralized systems, institutions can better manage their exposure to digital assets and navigate the evolving regulatory landscape.
- Decentralized finance (DeFi) applications: Decentralized custody solutions can play a crucial role in the broader DeFi ecosystem, providing secure storage and management for assets used in lending, borrowing, trading, and other financial applications.

- Cross-chain asset management: As the digital asset ecosystem becomes increasingly fragmented across multiple blockchains, decentralized custody solutions can help to bridge the gap between different networks and enable seamless asset management across a diverse range of platforms.
- Digital identity and access control: Decentralized custody solutions can also be used to manage digital identities and control access to sensitive information or services. By leveraging cryptographic keys and multi-signature schemes, these solutions can provide a secure and privacy-preserving way to authenticate users and verify their credentials.

5.7.5 Challenges and Future Outlook

While decentralized custody solutions offer significant potential for reshaping the digital asset landscape, they also face a number of challenges and uncertainties. These include:

- Regulatory uncertainty: The legal status of decentralized custody solutions remains unclear in many jurisdictions, and future regulatory developments could have a significant impact on their adoption and use. It will be crucial for the industry to engage with regulators and policymakers to ensure that these solutions can continue to evolve in a compliant and sustainable manner.
- User experience and adoption: Decentralized custody solutions can be more complex and difficult to use than their centralized counterparts, which may present barriers to adoption for less tech-savvy users. Improving the user experience and simplifying the onboarding process will be essential for driving mainstream adoption of these solutions.
- Interoperability and standardization: As the digital asset ecosystem continues to grow and diversify, it will be increasingly important for decentralized custody solutions to support a wide range of assets and platforms. This will require ongoing efforts to develop cross-chain interoperability solutions and establish industry standards for asset management and security.
- Security risks: While decentralized custody solutions offer a higher level of security than centralized systems, they are not immune to hacks, fraud, and other forms of compromise. Ensuring the ongoing security and resilience of these solutions will be a critical challenge for the industry as it continues to evolve.

In conclusion, decentralized custody solutions represent a new paradigm in digital asset management, offering a more secure, transparent, and flexible alternative to traditional custodial services. As the digital asset ecosystem continues to mature, these solutions have the potential to play a crucial role in shaping the future of finance and empowering individuals and institutions alike to take greater control over their financial lives.

5.8 The Most Secure Crypto Custody Model

Crypto Assets: Safeguarding Your Digital Fortune

When it comes to crypto assets, custody is all about keeping your valuable digital treasures secure and well-managed. It involves protecting the confidential, integral, and accessible cryptographic keys that lie at the heart of blockchain transactions. The security of custody is paramount because if those keys are lost, so are your funds—unless we're talking about certain tokenized assets.

Choosing the right custody model is like picking a strategy to handle this important task. It's a multifaceted concept that should align perfectly with an organization's operating model and risk management approach. Let's dive into the three main dimensions of custody.

Self-Custody or Sub-Custody?

The big decision boils down to doing it yourself or delegating the responsibility:

- Self-custody means you retain full control over your assets—you're the only one who knows the keys. No need to trust a third party. But remember, with great control comes great responsibility. You'll be in charge of defining and executing all security procedures, and if things go wrong, you'll have no one to blame but yourself. Some folks advocate for this approach with the saying "not your keys, not your coins," but let's not forget the other side: "lose your keys, lose your coins."

- Sub-custody involves placing your trust in a specialized organization that excels in digital asset custody. They'll store your funds and provide you with tools to manage them, like web interfaces for initiating transfers. If you choose this route, it's crucial to conduct due diligence and properly assess the risks. How likely is the custodian to go bankrupt? What internal controls do they have in place to mitigate insider risks? You'll be dealing with counterparty risk.

Deciding between self-custody and sub-custody depends on your unique situation. If you're a bank or a large corporation, self-custody is usually the way to go since handling and managing assets is your bread and butter. You have the necessary expertise in risk regulations and auditing protocols. For financial services firms like investment funds or brokers, self-custody is recommended if you have the right staff, expertise, and overall readiness to manage a custody system.

But remember, self-custody doesn't mean reinventing the wheel and building your own custody technology. In most cases, those who choose self-custody rely on third-party solutions like Taurus-PROTECT. Self-custody eliminates counterparty risk, allows you to control your product roadmap, ensures privacy (unlike sub-custodians who can see all flows), and optimizes your business case with higher margins.

If you're an individual or a smaller, less-regulated entity, sub-custody may be a better option from a risk management perspective. Just make sure you partner with a reliable sub-custody provider. Choosing such a provider can be tricky in the volatile and partially regulated cryptocurrency space.

Hybrid Custody: Sharing Control

In some cases, control of keys is distributed among multiple parties in what we call hybrid custody models. This typically involves the asset owner and a service provider using multi-party signing protocols. With such setups, only the owner maintains full control of the funds through their backup recovery values. Multi-signature models also fall under the hybrid category, as governance and control of funds are enforced cryptographically, preventing any single entity from unilaterally initiating transactions.

Hot or Cold?

Loosely speaking, a hot wallet refers to a custody system that is easily accessible and directly connected to the internet. On the other hand, a cold wallet is offline and involves more manual steps, making it safer against theft, especially software vulnerabilities and phishing attacks.

- Hot: Transactions can be automatically performed via API with approval from one or multiple systems through quorum-approval models.
- Warm: Transactions require manual approval from human parties. These approvals are transmitted to a secure environment that verifies them, creates blockchain transactions, and broadcasts them to the network.
- Cold: The environment holding the keys is physically disconnected from any computer network. Finalizing a transaction requires hands-on intervention following proper approvals and access procedures.

In all these setups, master keys or "seeds" are stored in hardware security modules (HSMs) with secure memory that offers high security assurance against various attacks, including physical ones. Some "cryogenic" setups even rely on non-digital systems to store keys in safe locations.

Managing fund distribution when dealing with different wallet temperatures can be challenging. A general rule of thumb is to keep the majority of funds in cold storage and only keep enough in hot and warm wallets for day-to-day operations, along with a buffer for handling withdrawal peaks. Processes should be in place to shuffle funds between wallet types, execute emergency transfers from cold storage (e.g., as a stop-loss mechanism), and retrieve backups from each wallet type.

Pooled or Allocated?

Lastly, let's address the question of funds pooling. If you're a bank managing your clients' assets, you have two main options:

- Pooled Model: All assets under custody are stored in the same "bucket," such as using the same Bitcoin address for all bitcoins. The bank maintains an internal record of each client's balances alongside a ledger of transaction history. This model is commonly used by cryptocurrency exchanges.
- Allocated Model: Each client's funds are assigned to distinct addresses, segregating them from each other. The bank would have different Bitcoin addresses for each client. These addresses can either belong to the same "tree" of addresses or have completely independent private keys.

Each model has its legal nuances, risk considerations, and operational constraints. There are many variations beyond these two basic models, shaped by the custodian's activities and the unique characteristics of each blockchain and asset type. For more details, refer to CMTA's Digital Assets Custody Standards (DACS) in §2.2 (note that these "pools" are different from mining pools).

Conclusion

No matter which custody model suits your organization best, its security level can range from excellent to abysmal based on how diligently you handle its risks. One common oversight is underestimating the risk of losing access to funds compared to theft risks. Many individuals and organizations have fallen victim to losing their assets due to inadequate backups or insufficient testing.

For financial institutions, the most secure custody solution involves a self-custody system that offers:

- Trustworthy technology from reputable providers with battle-tested solutions.
- Comprehensive risk management encompassing governance, security controls, and audit considerations.

Safeguarding the crypto assets requires careful consideration and proactive measures to ensure their long-term security.

5.9 Learned Lessons: Avoiding Digital Asset Storage Disasters - Insights from 5 Crypto Custody Failures

In the realm of digital asset wallets, true ownership and control stem from the knowledge of a secret value. This value, represented by a seemingly random string like "8f7a2e6b1d503c9a2b4e8f5c0a7d6b91" holds the key to accessing all the private keys within numerous wallets. While it is recommended to use a 256-bit secret, 128-bit secrets are more commonly used.

The significance of this secret cannot be understated. If someone were to discover it, they would have the power to pilfer all your cryptocurrency. To mitigate this risk, consumer wallets often employ "seed phrases" or "mnemonics" as per the BIP39 standard. These phrases, such as "version source detect result mammal galaxy lunar process woman disease bomb margin," are equivalent to the raw secret and possess the same level of uncertainty, or entropy, at 128 bits.

Now, you may wonder about the difficulty of "guessing" this value. Let's put it into perspective. There are a staggering 2^{128} (or approximately 3.4×10^{38}) possible 128-bit strings. Trying them one by one until stumbling upon the correct one is simply impractical due to the immense magnitude of this number. To give you an idea, 2^{128} is a billion times larger than 2^{88}, which roughly represents the age of the universe in nanoseconds (with a billion nanoseconds in a second).

However, exhaustive search or brute force is not the only method for stealing secret keys. Cryptographers have identified various other ways to accomplish this nefarious task. The primary goal of a crypto custody solution is to thwart such attacks, even from well-funded and patient attackers. Unfortunately, the history of crypto custody is marred by notable failures, be it through sub-custodians like exchanges or self-custody. Let's delve into five remarkable crypto custody disasters and examine how attacker ingenuity, inadequate security controls, and unfortunate circumstances often converge.

Please note that we have opted not to discuss TAURUS-related incidents and have excluded DeFi-related security breaches, flash loan attacks, and smart contract bugs from our scope. For more information on these specific incidents, you can refer to the provided sources. Additionally, we have chosen not to mention the FTX or LUNA tragedies as improper custody was not their primary issue, although it did contribute to their overall problems.

Disaster 1: Coincheck Exchange Hack (2018)

In January 2018, Coincheck, a Tokyo-based cryptocurrency exchange, fell victim to one of the most significant crypto thefts in history. Attackers successfully stole 523 million NEM tokens (XEM) from Coincheck's hot wallet, amounting to around $530 million at that time. Coincheck later compensated affected customers for their losses.

This high-profile breach prompted intense scrutiny from regulators and the wider community. In response, Coincheck temporarily halted withdrawals and deposits for most cryptocurrencies. Over subsequent weeks, the company worked tirelessly to identify the culprits and unravel the intricacies of the attack. Ultimately, it became apparent that the hackers exploited a vulnerability in Coincheck's access control protocols to gain access to their hot wallet.

This incident prompted Japan's Financial Services Agency (FSA) to tighten regulations governing cryptocurrency exchanges operating within the country. As part of their recovery efforts, Coincheck was eventually acquired by Monex Group, a Japanese online brokerage, with the aim of rebuilding and compensating affected users.

It's worth noting that Coincheck's hack is not an isolated case; numerous exchange platforms have suffered breaches and fund losses. As we write this, we have just learned about HTX's (formerly Huobi) $8 million loss due to a hack. Online resources provide various lists documenting exchange hacks.

Root Causes:

- Lack of cold storage: Coincheck stored a significant amount of NEM in a hot wallet connected to the internet instead of a more secure cold wallet isolated from online access.
- Weak approval measures: The exchange utilized single-signature wallets without a multi-party approval protocol. This allowed attackers to issue transactions from the hot wallet interface with compromise of a single system. Additionally, there seemed to be no robust whitelisting mechanism in place.
- Weak detection measures: No measures were implemented to detect and block unauthorized transactions. Best practices include setting limits on asset transfers within transactions or over specific time periods.

Disaster 2: QuadrigaCX Exchange Failure (2019)

In 2019, QuadrigaCX, a Canadian cryptocurrency exchange, faced a severe crisis following the sudden death of its CEO, Gerald Cotten. Unfortunately, Cotten was the sole individual with access to users' funds stored in cold wallets and had not shared the necessary access keys. Consequently, approximately $190 million worth of cryptocurrencies became inaccessible after his demise.

In response, QuadrigaCX filed for creditor protection, triggering investigations and legal proceedings. Ultimately, the exchange was declared bankrupt with insufficient assets to cover users' losses. As of May 2023, the law firm representing QuadrigaCX creditors announced a 13 percent reimbursement for each verified claim based on a 2019 valuation of their initial investments.

To delve deeper into this story, you may want to watch the documentary film available on Netflix.

Root Causes:

Single point of control: Gerald Cotten held exclusive access to QuadrigaCX's cold wallets containing substantial cryptocurrency funds. This created a central point of control and failure as only Cotten could execute fund transfers without supervision or third-party approval.

Lack of contingency planning: No backup or recovery measures were in place if Cotten became incapacitated or unable to access the funds.

Inadequate operational security: Funds were reportedly transferred to personal accounts without proper segregation of duties or internal checks and balances.

Poor financial management: The company lacked proper accounting and financial tracking mechanisms exacerbated by reliance on multiple third-party payment processors due to banking issues.

Delayed communication and transparency: Following Cotten's death, there was a delay in informing customers and regulators about liquidity issues, leading to increased mistrust and speculation. As of 2023, several aspects of the QuadrigaCX case remain unresolved.

Disaster 3: Wormhole Bridge Hack (2022)

In February 2022, an attacker exploited a vulnerability in the Wormhole token bridge, resulting in the loss of 120,000 Wrapped Ether (wETH) tokens valued at over $320 million at that time. wETH is a separate token from Ethereum's native cryptocurrency (ETH) and facilitates its use on other blockchains. Ideally, wETH should hold equivalent value to ETH.

A bridge serves as a protocol implemented through smart contract programs that connect two blockchains by allowing the same asset (e.g., ETH) to exist as distinct tokens on both chains. When moving Ether from Ethereum to Solana via such a bridge, it locks the original ETH and mints wETH on Solana. What could possibly go wrong?

Wormhole stands as a popular bridge linking Ethereum and Solana blockchains while also functioning as a token and NFT bridge. In this incident, the hacker minted 120,000 wETH on Solana without providing an equivalent amount on Ethereum due to a subtle flaw in Wormhole's smart contract code. Specifically, there was an incomplete validation of privileged accounts as detailed in Kudelski Security's analysis.

Root Causes:

Inherent risks associated with bridges: Bridges entail complex logic involving multiple blockchains and often possess token-holding and minting capabilities. Security attention may vary across different bridges. Wormhole is not the sole bridge that has experienced hacking incidents.

Smart contract security challenges: Securing smart contracts proves challenging, especially for non-trivial ones like bridge contracts. Subtle flaws can lead to catastrophic and irreversible consequences, with recovery from an exploit being far from simple compared to patching code in web applications. In the Wormhole case, the bug stemmed from an incomplete validation of privileged accounts due to deprecated function usage. This allowed the attacker to impersonate these accounts and mint tokens with their privilege levels.

6 Compliance and Regulatory Considerations

6.1 Navigating the Digital Frontier: An Introduction to Compliance in Digital Asset Custody

In the early days of digital assets, the landscape resembled a modern-day Wild West: a vast, open space brimming with opportunity, innovation, and with its fair share of challenges. As with any pioneering venture, the early actors on this digital frontier operated with limited oversight, guided by a vision of decentralization and unfettered by traditional bureaucratic processes.

But as the digital asset ecosystem has matured, so has the necessity for clear rules, guidelines, and frameworks to ensure safety, trustworthiness, and stability. Thus, the world of compliance in digital asset custody was born, marrying the novel and disruptive power of digital assets with the foundational principles of traditional financial systems.

Comprehending the Need for Compliance

To understand compliance's role in digital asset custody, one must first grasp the unique challenges presented by digital assets. Unlike traditional assets, which have centuries of regulatory, legal, and societal frameworks built around them, digital assets are a recent invention. Their digital nature, global reach, and decentralized ethos pose both risks and rewards.

For instance, digital assets introduce new paradigms such as cryptographic ownership, trustless transactions, and decentralized control. While these innovations offer numerous benefits, they also introduce challenges like potential loss of assets due to lost cryptographic keys, susceptibility to hacking, and regulatory arbitrage.

Global Traction and Regulatory Attention

As digital assets gained traction worldwide, regulators took note. The increased adoption of cryptocurrencies and subsequent initial coin offerings (ICOs) in the mid-2010s drew significant media and public attention. High-profile hacks, frauds, and the potential for money laundering only intensified the spotlight on this burgeoning domain. With billions of dollars and consumer interests at stake, the need for a regulatory framework became clear.

Compliance: A Trust Bridge Between Two Worlds

In many ways, the advent of compliance in the realm of digital asset custody has been a boon for the entire industry. For traditional investors, the presence of compliance and regulatory oversight serves as a bridge of trust, assuring them that digital assets, despite their novel nature, can be as secure and trustworthy as traditional investments.

From the perspective of digital asset innovators, compliance ensures that their innovations can integrate into the broader financial ecosystem. It provides a roadmap for ensuring that while these assets redefine the future of finance, they do so responsibly.

Key Tenets of Compliance in Digital Asset Custody

There are several foundational principles to understand when considering compliance in this space:

- Asset Protection: At the heart of custody is the protection of assets. Regulations ensure that custodians implement robust security measures to safeguard clients' assets.
- Transparency: Compliance mandates that custodians provide clear, consistent, and transparent reporting, ensuring that stakeholders have an accurate view of their holdings and transactions.
- Consumer Protection: Given the complexity of digital assets, regulatory frameworks also emphasize consumer protection, ensuring that even those unfamiliar with the intricacies of blockchain technology are not taken advantage of.
- Anti-Money Laundering (AML) and Counter-Terrorist Financing (CTF): Regulators worldwide are keen to ensure that the digital asset ecosystem is not a conduit for illicit funds. This emphasis means custodians must implement rigorous checks and transaction monitoring systems.

The Ongoing Evolution of Compliance

Digital asset compliance is not static. As the technology and industry evolve, so do the regulatory requirements. Regulators worldwide grapple with the challenges of overseeing a rapidly changing domain while ensuring that their nations benefit from digital assets' promise.

In places like the European Union and the United States, we've seen dynamic shifts in the regulatory landscape. From discussions around security vs. utility tokens to frameworks around stablecoins and central bank digital currencies (CBDCs), the dialogue continues to evolve.

Conclusion

Navigating the digital frontier of asset custody requires more than just technical prowess; it necessitates a deep understanding of the broader societal, financial, and regulatory implications of these novel assets. Compliance, with its emphasis on security, transparency, and responsibility, ensures that as we journey into this new frontier, we do so with a map and compass in hand.

6.2 Jurisdictional Variances: A Global Compliance Puzzle

The global nature of digital assets is one of their most defining, and yet, challenging attributes. As decentralized currencies without borders, they are naturally poised to transcend regional limitations. However, while the digital ledger on which these assets reside might be universal, the regulatory landscapes they traverse are anything but. Each nation, informed by its economic priorities, cultural nuances, and historical context, views and regulates digital assets differently.

A Historical Perspective

Traditionally, when financial instruments or new forms of investments have been introduced to the market, their reception has been primarily regional. Think of the European joint-stock companies of the 17th century or the US junk bond phenomena of the 1980s. Yet, digital assets exploded on the global stage almost simultaneously, leaving regulators worldwide scrambling to understand and manage them.

Key Regions and Their Stances

To appreciate the global puzzle that digital asset compliance presents, let's examine the regulatory landscapes of a few major regions as of 2023:

- United States: The US regulatory environment has been characterized by a sectoral approach. Multiple agencies, including the SEC (Securities and Exchange Commission), CFTC (Commodity Futures Trading Commission), and FinCEN (Financial Crimes Enforcement Network), have stakes in the game. For instance, while the SEC views some tokens as securities, the CFTC treats cryptocurrencies like commodities. This multiplicity sometimes results in ambiguity but also provides a thoroughness of oversight.
- European Union: The EU, under the guidance of the European Securities and Markets Authority (ESMA), has been proactive in addressing digital assets. They've been keen on drawing a distinction between 'utility' tokens (which provide users with a future access to a product) and 'security' tokens (akin to traditional securities). With the introduction of MiCA (Markets in Crypto-assets Regulation), the EU aims to provide a comprehensive regulatory framework for crypto-assets.
- Asia: This region is a mosaic of regulatory responses:
- China: Once home to the majority of Bitcoin mining, China has taken a strict stance against ICOs and cryptocurrency exchanges, though it has embraced blockchain technology and is piloting its digital yuan.
- Japan: Recognizing Bitcoin as legal tender in 2017, Japan is one of the more progressive Asian countries regarding digital asset regulation, with a strong emphasis on consumer protection.
- Singapore: The Monetary Authority of Singapore (MAS) has been relatively open to digital assets, focusing on robust AML and CTF regulations.
- Emerging Economies: Many countries, like India and South Africa, are grappling with the promise and challenges of digital assets. While recognizing the potential benefits of blockchain technology and financial inclusivity, they also grapple with concerns about capital flight, AML risks, and economic sovereignty.

The Challenge of Harmonization

Given these diverse regulatory approaches, one of the main challenges for global entities operating in the digital asset custody space is harmonization. Ensuring that a digital asset platform adheres to the regulations of every jurisdiction it operates in is no small feat. For instance, what qualifies as a permissible marketing communication for a token in one country might be deemed a non-compliant securities solicitation in another.

Jurisdictional Arbitrage: A Double-Edged Sword

A consequence of these variances is the rise of jurisdictional arbitrage. Many digital asset projects strategically locate their operations in countries with favorable regulatory climates. While this can spur innovation and foster a welcoming environment for nascent technologies, it also raises concerns about "race-to-the-bottom" dynamics, where entities migrate to the least restrictive jurisdictions, potentially compromising consumer protection and systemic oversight.

A Look Ahead

As digital assets continue to mature, the need for international regulatory collaboration becomes evident. Global forums like the G20 and international bodies like the Financial Action Task Force (FATF) are increasingly focusing on creating harmonized standards for digital assets.

Conclusion

Navigating the intricate tapestry of global digital asset regulations is a formidable challenge for any custodial entity. The key lies in striking a balance: ensuring robust compliance without stifling innovation, protecting consumers without curbing the democratizing potential of digital assets, and fostering global collaboration while respecting national sovereignty.

6.3 KYC and AML Protocols in the Digital Age

In the grand scheme of the digital asset realm, there's an overarching concern that goes beyond the mere custody and transaction of these assets: ensuring their legitimacy. Two pillars stand robustly in this realm, fortifying the space against misuse and exploitation - Know Your Customer (KYC) and Anti-Money Laundering (AML) protocols. These measures have long been integral to traditional finance, but as we shift into the digital age, their implementation, challenges, and implications take on new dimensions.

Traditional KYC and AML: A Brief Overview

Understanding KYC and AML's nuances in the context of digital assets first requires a grasp of their traditional forms:

- Know Your Customer (KYC): Rooted in the principle of understanding the identity and intention of a financial institution's clients, KYC protocols traditionally involve verifying personal identification details, assessing client risk, and monitoring transactions.
- Anti-Money Laundering (AML): A broader framework, AML encompasses policies, laws, and regulations aiming to prevent financial systems from being used to launder illicit funds, finance terrorism, or engage in corrupt activities.

The Digital Shift: New Opportunities, New Challenges

Digital assets, by design, introduce a paradox. On one end, they offer greater transparency with immutable ledgers and transaction histories. On the other, pseudonymity is foundational to many digital asset protocols. This dual nature presents both opportunities and challenges for KYC and AML implementations.

- Pseudonymous Transactions: Unlike anonymous transactions, which hide identity entirely, pseudonymous ones involve an alias. In the context of most blockchain networks, public keys serve as these aliases. While transactions are transparent, linking them to real-world identities isn't straightforward.
- Cross-border Transactions: Digital assets are inherently global. This nature, while revolutionary, complicates compliance. A Bitcoin sent from Japan to Brazil traverses no checkpoints, unlike traditional cross-border transfers.
- Diverse Asset Types: Beyond the realm of cryptocurrencies lie tokens representing a plethora of assets, from real estate to artwork. Verifying the legitimacy of these assets and ensuring they're not used for illicit activities introduces another layer of complexity.

Modern KYC in the Digital Asset Arena

The digitization of KYC has introduced various tools and techniques optimized for the digital asset space:

- Digital Identity Verification: Traditional paper-based ID checks have transitioned to more robust digital verification methods, leveraging AI and machine learning. Advanced systems now can scan government IDs, match them with real-time video or photo scans of users, and even detect potential deepfakes.
- Behavioral Analysis: Advanced platforms assess a user's transaction behavior over time. Deviations from the norm can trigger alerts, allowing compliance teams to investigate potential illicit activities.
- Risk Profiling: Given the vast ecosystem of digital assets, not all assets are created equal. Modern KYC systems can categorize assets based on their risk profiles. For instance, tokens from a recent, unaudited ICO might be deemed riskier than well-established cryptocurrencies.

AML Protocols for the Next Generation

In the face of evolving challenges, AML protocols for digital assets have seen revolutionary shifts:

- Chain Analysis: Several platforms now provide detailed analytics of blockchain transactions, tracing funds' origins and destinations. Such tools can detect patterns associated with darknet markets, ransomware, or other illicit activities.
- Decentralized Exchanges and DeFi: Decentralized platforms, which operate without intermediaries, pose significant AML challenges. Monitoring such ecosystems requires new tools that can interact with smart contracts, understand token swaps, and assess liquidity pools.
- Smart Contract Audits: AML in the age of Ethereum and other smart contract platforms also involves auditing the contract code itself. Ensuring that contracts don't facilitate money laundering, especially in complex DeFi constructs, is crucial.

Global Collaborations and Regulatory Harmonization

Given digital assets' global nature, no single jurisdiction can tackle the associated KYC and AML challenges alone. International collaboration, shared standards, and mutual learning are the need of the hour. Forums like the Financial Action Task Force (FATF) play crucial roles in this endeavor, providing guidelines that member countries can adapt and adopt.

Looking Ahead

While the tools, techniques, and challenges of KYC and AML in the digital realm might differ from their traditional counterparts, their core objective remains unchanged: ensuring the integrity of financial systems. As digital assets continue to reshape finance, the intertwined dance between innovation and regulation will undoubtedly persist, challenging and enhancing both domains in the process.

6.4 Regulatory Sandboxes: Encouraging Innovation While Ensuring Compliance

As the sun rises on the digital era, it casts long shadows on the regulatory landscape, highlighting the tension between innovation and compliance. Traditional regulatory mechanisms, designed for a slower-paced financial world, risk stifling the rapid innovation emblematic of the digital asset space. Enter regulatory sandboxes: a novel approach that seeks to reconcile this tension, allowing innovation to flourish under the watchful eyes of regulators.

Setting the Stage: The Need for a New Approach

To comprehend the rise of regulatory sandboxes, it's essential to understand the unique challenges posed by digital assets:

- Rapid Evolution: The pace of technological development in the digital asset realm far outstrips that of traditional finance. New platforms, tokens, and financial mechanisms emerge almost daily, challenging existing regulatory frameworks.

- Technological Complexity: The intricacies of blockchain technology, cryptographic protocols, and smart contracts aren't always immediately apparent. Regulators need time and expertise to understand these innovations before they can draft relevant regulations.
- Global Nature: Digital assets don't respect national boundaries. Their decentralized and global character poses challenges for regulators accustomed to national or regional jurisdictions.

Given these challenges, there's a clear need for a regulatory approach that's flexible, agile, and informed.

What is a Regulatory Sandbox?

At its core, a regulatory sandbox is a structured environment wherein innovators can test new financial products, services, models, or delivery mechanisms without immediately incurring all the regulatory consequences of these activities. It's akin to a child playing in a sandbox, constructing castles and moats in a controlled environment, under the watchful eyes of guardians, ensuring that the broader playground remains safe.

The Appeal of the Sandbox

For Innovators:

- Safe Environment to Test: Innovators get a risk-reduced space to test their products and services without fear of unintended regulatory violations.
- Feedback Loop: Direct interaction with regulators provides valuable feedback, guiding refinements and ensuring eventual compliance.
- Faster Time-to-Market: Reduced initial regulatory hurdles can expedite product launches.

For Regulators:

- Learning Opportunity: Regulators gain insights into emerging technologies and business models.
- Preemptive Oversight: It's easier to guide a product in its nascent stages than to regulate it post-launch.
- Global Benchmarking: Sandboxes allow regulators to stay abreast of global best practices, ensuring their national markets remain competitive.

Notable Implementations

Several jurisdictions worldwide have embraced the sandbox approach:

Here is an updated summary that includes information on the European Union's approach to regulatory sandboxes:

As of 2023, many jurisdictions around the world have adopted regulatory sandboxes to support fintech innovation, including the European Union:

- United Kingdom: The UK's Financial Conduct Authority launched the first regulatory sandbox in 2016. The FCA's sandbox has inspired many other countries to launch their own sandboxes.

- European Union: The EU launched a bloc-wide fintech sandbox in 2021 to harmonize rules across member states. The EU sandbox allows startups to test products and services across multiple countries. This helps address the challenge of navigating different regulations in each member state.

- Singapore: The Monetary Authority of Singapore operates the Fintech Regulatory Sandbox. Singapore is a major fintech hub, and MAS actively uses the sandbox to guide startups in developing products and services for the Asian market.

- Switzerland: The Swiss Financial Market Supervisory Authority (FINMA) launched a fintech sandbox in 2017. Switzerland is working to establish itself as a center for blockchain and digital asset startups, and the FINMA sandbox plays an important role.

- Thailand: The Bank of Thailand launched a regulatory sandbox for fintechs in 2017. Thailand aims to become a fintech leader in Southeast Asia, and its central bank is taking an active role in enabling innovation.

- Malaysia: Bank Negara Malaysia, the country's central bank, started a fintech regulatory sandbox in 2016. Malaysia is fostering a pro-business environment for fintechs and aims to make Kuala Lumpur a leading fintech hub.

- Hong Kong: The Hong Kong Monetary Authority launched a fintech sandbox in 2017. As a major financial center, Hong Kong aims to enable responsible fintech innovation that can serve local and international markets.

- Australia: The Australian Securities and Investments Commission operates a regulatory sandbox for fintech startups. Australia is working to revamp its financial regulations to promote innovation and support new technologies like blockchain.

- Canada: The Canadian Securities Administrators launched a regulatory sandbox initiative in cooperation with several provincial regulators. Canada aims to establish itself as a center for fintech and is revising rules to be more flexible toward innovation.

- Brazil: The Central Bank of Brazil launched a regulatory sandbox for fintechs in 2018. Brazil's government aims to drive innovation in financial services to promote greater access and efficiency. The central bank sandbox plays an important role in enabling new products and services.

- Russia: The Bank of Russia set up a regulatory sandbox for fintech startups in 2018. Russia aims to build a digital economy and sees fintech innovation as an important driver of growth and competitiveness. The central bank sandbox helps guide startups in this effort.

So in summary, regulatory sandboxes have been embraced in many of the world's leading financial hubs, emerging fintech markets, and by the European Union. Overall, sandboxes reflect a willingness by governments and regulators to support innovation that can expand access to financial services and drive economic growth. For fintech startups, sandboxes provide an opportunity to tap into new markets by working closely with regulators to ensure products and services comply with local rules.

Challenges and Critiques

While the sandbox approach offers many benefits, it's not without its challenges:

- Scalability Issues: As the number of applications to these programs grows, regulators may find it challenging to allocate adequate resources and attention to each project.
- Potential for Bias: There's a risk that regulators might favor certain types of projects or inadvertently promote specific business models over others.
- Lack of Guarantees: Graduating from a sandbox doesn't always guarantee long-term regulatory compliance, especially if broader regulations evolve.

Looking Ahead: The Future of Regulatory Sandboxes

The digital landscape is ever-evolving, and regulatory sandboxes, by design, are adaptable frameworks. As more jurisdictions embrace this approach and as more projects graduate from these programs, the global financial ecosystem will benefit from a rich tapestry of case studies and learned lessons. Collaborations between countries, sharing insights, successes, and failures, will be crucial.

Moreover, as the line between digital and traditional finance continues to blur, the principles behind regulatory sandboxes might inform broader regulatory philosophies, shaping a more flexible, responsive, and innovation-friendly financial future.

Conclusion

In the dynamic dance between innovation and regulation, the regulatory sandbox emerges as a harmonizing force. By providing a structured, safe environment for experimentation, it ensures that the digital asset realm can continue its groundbreaking journey, with the assurance that the path ahead considers consumer safety, market integrity, and the spirit of innovation in equal measure.

6.5 The Crucial Role of Reporting: Transparency, Audits, and Digital Assets

In the digital asset universe, where trust is distributed and transactions are irreversible, transparency is not just a luxury; it's a necessity. Reporting, in this realm, becomes the beacon of trust, shining light on operations, ensuring stakeholders that everything is as it should be. But with digital assets, the game has changed, and so have the rules of reporting. Let's delve into this evolved landscape.

Traditional Reporting: A Brief Retrospective

To appreciate the nuances of reporting in the digital asset realm, it's worth revisiting its traditional counterparts:

- Financial Reporting: Companies are required to disclose their financial position periodically, typically in the form of quarterly and annual reports. This gives stakeholders an understanding of the company's health and direction.
- Compliance Reporting: Financial institutions report to regulatory bodies, ensuring they comply with the law, be it Anti-Money Laundering (AML) regulations, Know Your Customer (KYC) protocols, or other rules.

- Audit: Independent bodies scrutinize these reports and the processes that generate them, ensuring their accuracy and reliability.

The Digital Asset Divergence

While the principles of transparency and trust remain unchanged, digital assets introduce unique challenges and opportunities:

- Immutability: Once recorded, blockchain transactions cannot be altered. This provides a level of assurance but also underscores the importance of precision.
- Pseudonymity: Public ledgers provide transaction transparency, but participants are often pseudonymous, represented by cryptographic addresses.
- Decentralization: With no central authority overseeing operations, ensuring transparency becomes both more challenging and more crucial.

Transparency in Digital Asset Transactions

Digital assets live on public ledgers, accessible to anyone with an internet connection. This degree of transparency is unprecedented:

- Real-time Reporting: Unlike traditional systems where reports are generated periodically, digital asset transactions are visible in real-time.
- Proof of Solvency: In the wake of several high-profile digital asset losses, some platforms offer "proof of solvency" reports, demonstrating they possess the assets they claim.
- Token Governance: Many digital asset platforms have native tokens, which give holders governance rights. Transparent reporting ensures these stakeholders can make informed decisions.

Auditing in the Age of Digital Assets

Traditional audits involve scrutinizing ledgers, receipts, and databases. But how does one audit a decentralized, immutable blockchain?

- Chain Analysis: Auditors can use tools to analyze blockchain data, tracing the origin and destination of funds.
- Cryptographic Proofs: Instead of showing each transaction, a custodian can provide a cryptographic proof of their holdings.
- Smart Contract Audits: Many digital assets and platforms rely on smart contracts. These aren't just audited for financial accuracy but for code vulnerabilities.

Regulatory Reporting

As regulators around the world grapple with the implications of digital assets, their reporting requirements are evolving:

- Transaction Reporting: Regulatory bodies in several jurisdictions require exchanges and custodians to report large or suspicious transactions, much like traditional financial institutions.
- Tax Implications: Tax authorities have introduced guidelines for reporting digital asset transactions, gains, and losses.
- Cross-Border Transactions: Given the global nature of digital assets, transactions that cross national borders might need to be reported to multiple regulatory bodies.

The Interplay of Privacy and Transparency

One of the most delicate balancing acts in the digital asset realm is between transparency and privacy:

- Private Transactions: Some digital assets, like Zcash or Monero, emphasize transaction privacy. Reporting and auditing these presents unique challenges.
- Data Protection Regulations: In jurisdictions with stringent data protection laws, like the EU with its GDPR, ensuring compliance while providing transparency becomes complex.

The Road Ahead: Innovations in Reporting and Auditing

The digital asset ecosystem is dynamic, and so are its reporting and auditing mechanisms:

- Decentralized Audits: Just as the assets themselves are decentralized, we might see the rise of decentralized auditing mechanisms, where a community, rather than a centralized body, validates reports.
- AI and Reporting: Machine learning algorithms could be used to detect anomalous patterns in transaction data, flagging potential issues.
- Integrated Platforms: As the ecosystem matures, we might see integrated platforms that automate much of the reporting process, pulling data directly from blockchains and other sources.

In Conclusion

In the ever-evolving world of digital assets, the adage "trust, but verify" has never been more relevant. Reporting, in this landscape, serves as both a tool of verification and a foundation for trust. As the sector continues to grow, the pioneers who prioritize transparency, backed by robust reporting and auditing mechanisms, will likely lead the charge, setting standards for the rest to follow.

6.6 Licensing Nuances: From Traditional Banking to Digital Asset Custodians

Navigating the labyrinthine world of financial regulation has never been a stroll in the park. Historically, traditional banks and financial institutions have danced to the tune of licenses that governed every facet of their operations. However, in the dawn of the digital age, digital asset custodians find themselves choreographing a new dance, as they grapple with licensing frameworks that are both familiar and profoundly different.

A Glimpse into Traditional Licensing

To shed light on the licensing nuances for digital assets, it's helpful to first journey through the legacy world:

- Banking Licenses: Banks traditionally need to acquire licenses to accept deposits, offer credit, or facilitate payments. These licenses ensure that institutions maintain sufficient reserves, follow ethical practices, and uphold fiduciary duties.
- Broker-Dealer Licenses: Institutions that buy and sell securities on behalf of others (or for themselves) need this license, subjecting them to a different set of regulatory obligations.
- Investment Advisor Registration: Financial entities that provide advice on securities investments or manage portfolios usually register as investment advisors.

Each of these licenses comes with its set of requirements, covering everything from minimum capital, to reporting standards, to consumer protection measures.

The Emergence of Digital Assets: A Regulatory Conundrum

Digital assets, by virtue of their decentralized, cryptographic, and global nature, defy easy categorization. Are they currencies? Securities? Commodities? This existential question has profound implications for licensing.

- Currency or Commodity?: If treated as currencies, digital assets might necessitate banking licenses for their custodians. But if considered commodities, a different regulatory regime might apply.
- Token Classifications: Not all digital tokens are born equal. Some function as utilities within a specific ecosystem, while others might represent shares in a project or entitle holders to dividends.
- Global yet Local: Digital assets operate on global networks, but regulations remain fiercely local. A custodian serving clients worldwide might need to grapple with myriad licensing regimes.

Licenses in the Digital Asset Universe

Given the distinctive characteristics of digital assets, many jurisdictions are carving out unique licensing paths for their custodians:

- BitLicenses: New York's Department of Financial Services introduced the "BitLicense" – a custom regulatory framework for digital asset businesses. This has been both lauded for its forward-thinking and critiqued for its stringent requirements.
- E-Money Licenses: In some European jurisdictions, digital asset custodians operate under e-money licenses, which allow them to hold and transfer client funds electronically.

- Special Banking Licenses: Some regions have introduced special banking licenses tailored for fintech and digital asset firms, ensuring that they can provide a range of financial services while still being regulated.

Case Study: The Swiss Approach

Switzerland, renowned for its banking legacy, offers a fascinating case study. The nation's regulators have introduced a dual licensing system for digital asset custodians:

- Banking License Lite: A less onerous banking license, tailored for fintech firms, which allows them to accept deposits but not engage in traditional banking activities.
- FINMA Guidelines: The Swiss Financial Market Supervisory Authority (FINMA) has laid out clear guidelines differentiating between payment, utility, and asset tokens, each with its regulatory implications.

This dual approach strikes a balance between innovation and regulation, ensuring consumer protection without stifling growth.

Navigating Multi-Jurisdictional Waters

For digital asset custodians operating across borders, the regulatory mosaic becomes particularly intricate:

- Harmonization Efforts: While each country retains its regulatory sovereignty, efforts are underway, especially within regions like the European Union, to harmonize digital asset regulations.
- Regulatory Arbitrage: Some firms strategically choose their headquarters based on favorable regulations, a phenomenon termed regulatory arbitrage.
- Global Standards: International bodies like the Financial Action Task Force (FATF) are working on global standards, especially concerning Anti-Money Laundering (AML) and Counter-Terrorist Financing (CTF) rules.

The Path Forward: Collaborative Regulation

Digital asset regulation and licensing are still in their formative stages, but a collaborative approach holds the key:

- Industry Lobbying: Digital asset industry bodies can play a crucial role in shaping favorable yet robust regulations.
- Regulatory Sandboxes: As discussed earlier, these provide a safe space for innovation while allowing regulators to understand and shape emerging technologies.
- Educative Initiatives: Both regulators and the industry can benefit from initiatives aimed at mutual education, facilitating a shared understanding.

In Conclusion

Licensing in the realm of digital asset custody is a dance on a tightrope, balancing the promise of groundbreaking innovation with the imperatives of security, transparency, and accountability. As regulators worldwide grapple with these nuances, it's clear that dialogue, collaboration, and a commitment to shared principles will light the way forward.

6.7 Decentralization vs. Regulation: Finding Common Ground

At the very heart of the digital asset revolution lies the principle of decentralization — the idea that power and control should be distributed rather than concentrated. It's a philosophy that resonates deeply within the blockchain community, challenging traditional centralized models of governance, finance, and even information flow. But as the sector grows and matures, it brushes up against regulatory frameworks built for a centralized world. This chapter unpacks this delicate dance between the decentralized ethos and the need for regulatory oversight in digital asset custody.

The Pillars of Decentralization

Understanding the push-and-pull between decentralization and regulation requires grounding in what decentralization truly entails:

- Elimination of Intermediaries: Decentralized systems aim to do away with middlemen, facilitating peer-to-peer interactions.
- Resilience and Redundancy: With no single point of failure, decentralized systems are inherently more resilient against attacks or failures.
- Empowerment and Autonomy: Decentralization seeks to give more control to individual participants, shifting away from top-down structures.

The Regulatory Imperative

Regulations in finance and many other sectors are built upon a few foundational principles:

- Consumer Protection: Ensuring that consumers are not subjected to fraud or malpractice and have recourse in cases of disputes.
- Maintaining Market Integrity: Ensuring that markets are transparent, stable, and not prone to manipulations.
- Preventing Illicit Activities: Stopping money laundering, terrorist financing, and other illegal activities.

The Points of Friction

Bringing these two worlds together is challenging, with several points of friction:

- Identity and Anonymity: Decentralized systems often prioritize user privacy, sometimes allowing for anonymous transactions. This contrasts sharply with regulatory requirements, especially concerning KYC (Know Your Customer) norms.
- Jurisdictional Challenges: Decentralized systems, by nature, do not adhere to geographical boundaries, making jurisdiction a complex issue.
- Responsibility and Liability: Without central intermediaries, it's challenging to determine where responsibility lies in cases of disputes or fraud.

Harmonizing the Two Philosophies

While friction exists, pioneers in the digital asset realm are exploring ways to harmonize decentralization with regulatory imperatives:

- Transparent Yet Private Transactions: Technologies like zero-knowledge proofs offer ways to verify transaction integrity without revealing transaction details, striking a balance between transparency and privacy.
- Decentralized Autonomous Organizations (DAOs) and Governance: DAOs, governed by consensus algorithms and smart contracts, offer a model where decentralized systems can still adhere to regulatory norms.
- Interoperable Compliance Protocols: Emerging standards allow decentralized systems to interact with traditional systems in a compliant manner, automating many compliance checks.

Case Study: The Evolution of Decentralized Exchanges

Decentralized exchanges (DEXs) offer a poignant example of this evolving relationship:

- Phase 1 — Pure Decentralization: Early DEXs were fully decentralized, with no central control. However, they often faced challenges with liquidity and regulatory compliance.
- Phase 2 — Hybrid Models: Recognizing these challenges, new DEXs emerged that combined decentralized trading with centralized components for compliance and liquidity management.
- Phase 3 — Decentralized Compliance: The next evolution might see DEXs leveraging technologies like decentralized oracles and AI-driven smart contracts to ensure compliance without central oversight.

Voices from the Industry

Engaging with key stakeholders offers further insights:

- The Regulator's Perspective: Many regulators emphasize that their primary concern isn't to stifle innovation but to ensure consumer protection and market integrity. They're open to understanding the benefits of decentralization and finding paths forward.
- The Innovator's View: Many in the blockchain community understand the importance of regulation. Their focus is on education — helping regulators understand the technology and its implications.

Navigating Future Pathways

As the digital asset realm grows, its relationship with regulators will undeniably evolve:

- Regulatory Sandboxes: As previously discussed, these offer a space where innovators can test new solutions under a relaxed regulatory framework.
- Global Collaboration: The borderless nature of blockchain necessitates a global regulatory approach. International forums and collaborations can help harmonize regulations across borders.
- Educating and Engaging: Continuous dialogue between the decentralized community and regulators will be vital. Workshops, conferences, and collaborative projects can bridge understanding gaps.

In Conclusion

Decentralization and regulation, at first glance, may seem at odds. However, both share underlying principles of fairness, transparency, and protection. The challenge and opportunity lie in building bridges of understanding and collaboration. As the digital asset landscape matures, it offers a unique canvas to reimagine governance and control, bringing the best of both worlds together.

6.8 Regulatory Challenges: Addressing Privacy Coins, Mixers, and Other Anonymity Tools

Introduction:

In recent years, privacy coins, mixers, and other anonymity tools have become increasingly popular among cryptocurrency users. While these tools can provide greater privacy and security for users, they also pose significant challenges for regulators and law enforcement agencies. In this section, we will explore the regulatory challenges associated with privacy coins, mixers, and other anonymity tools and discuss potential solutions.

Privacy Coins:

Privacy coins are cryptocurrencies that offer greater privacy and anonymity than traditional cryptocurrencies like Bitcoin. These coins use various techniques to obfuscate transaction details, making it more difficult for third parties to track transactions. While privacy coins can provide greater privacy for users, they also pose significant challenges for regulators and law enforcement agencies.

One of the main challenges associated with privacy coins is their potential use in illicit activities such as money laundering and terrorism financing. Because privacy coins make it difficult to track transactions, they can be used to facilitate illegal activities without detection. This poses a significant challenge for regulators who are tasked with preventing such activities.

To address these challenges, regulators may consider implementing stricter regulations around privacy coins. For example, they may require exchanges to perform enhanced due diligence on customers who use privacy coins or require exchanges to delist privacy coins altogether.

Mixers:

Mixers are tools that allow users to obfuscate the origin of their cryptocurrency transactions. These tools work by mixing together multiple transactions from different users, making it difficult to trace individual transactions back to their origin. While mixers can provide greater privacy for users, they also pose significant challenges for regulators and law enforcement agencies.

One of the main challenges associated with mixers is their potential use in money laundering and other illicit activities. Because mixers make it difficult to trace transactions back to their origin, they can be used to launder money or finance illegal activities without detection.

To address these challenges, regulators may consider implementing stricter regulations around mixers. For example, they may require exchanges to perform enhanced due diligence on customers who use mixers or require exchanges to delist cryptocurrencies that are frequently used with mixers.

Other Anonymity Tools:

In addition to privacy coins and mixers, there are other anonymity tools that cryptocurrency users can use to obfuscate their transactions. These tools include anonymizing networks like Tor and VPNs that can be used to hide a user's IP address. While these tools can provide greater privacy for users, they also pose significant challenges for regulators and law enforcement agencies.

One of the main challenges associated with these anonymity tools is their potential use in illegal activities such as money laundering and terrorism financing. Because these tools make it difficult to track transactions, they can be used to facilitate illegal activities without detection.

To address these challenges, regulators may consider implementing stricter regulations around anonymity tools. For example, they may require exchanges to perform enhanced due diligence on customers who use anonymity tools or require exchanges to delist cryptocurrencies that are frequently used with anonymity tools.

Conclusion:

Privacy coins, mixers, and other anonymity tools can provide greater privacy and security for cryptocurrency users, but they also pose significant challenges for regulators and law enforcement agencies. To address these challenges, regulators may consider implementing stricter regulations around these tools or requiring exchanges to perform enhanced due diligence on customers who use them. By balancing the need for privacy with the need for security, we can create a regulatory environment that supports innovation while also preventing illicit activities.

7 Risks on Digital Asset Custody

7.1 Introduction

Decentralized blockchain technology systems operate without a central control authority. Therefore, each user must comprehend their specific role, associated tasks, responsibilities, and related risks. The primary element through which a user conducts transactions and manages their cryptocurrency and digital assets is a private key. Consequently, effective "key management is crucial." If a user loses their private key, they cannot recover it from a central authority or request a new one. Restoring a private key is only possible with a suitable backup solution in place.

Providers of crypto custody solutions are service companies that offer secure storage options for cryptocurrencies. These solutions cater to both institutional and private clients, aiming to ensure the availability, confidentiality, and integrity (referred to as "protection goals") of private keys and the necessary information for their restoration (backups), enabling customers to access their cryptocurrencies.

7.2 Crypto custody risks

Private keys enable users to access their digital assets and protect against unauthorized access or transactions. Compromising a private key, for instance, through fraud or theft, could allow third parties to take control of the digital assets. Therefore, it's crucial to securely create and store private keys and their backups.

Some of the most significant risks for users involve the compromise of their private keys and backups, leading to a loss of confidentiality, availability, or integrity:

- Confidentiality: The risk of unauthorized individuals accessing private keys and backups, potentially allowing them to execute transactions and access digital assets.
- Availability: The risk that private keys and their backups may become inaccessible or delayed. If this occurs, accessing the digital assets might become impossible.
- Integrity: The risk that private keys or their backups may be altered and rendered unreadable, making it difficult to access the digital assets.

These primary risks give rise to additional risks during the main phases of a private key's life cycle:

- Key ceremony: Various risks exist during the key ceremony (when private keys are generated). For example, private keys may be viewed or copied during generation or while being transported to their ultimate storage location. These attacks can be perpetrated by individuals directly involved or by unauthorized persons gaining access to technical components.

105

- Key management: In managing private keys and their backups, inherent risks include potential loss, theft, or tampering. Lack of clear responsibilities for storage or failure to follow security protocols can also lead to fraud.
- Transactions: Initiating and approving transactions for digital assets can pose financial risks if the control system is inadequately designed or if duties are not properly segregated. Unlike traditional banking, errors or fraud in the crypto world may not be refundable.

Failure in cryptocurrency controls can also present significant risks from a financial statement perspective:

- Custodian: Loss of control over cryptocurrencies requires them to be derecognized as assets, with the loss booked on the income statement. The custodian typically retains liability towards the customer in such cases.
- Companies with cryptocurrencies on their balance sheet: Loss of control over these assets necessitates derecognition and booking the loss on the income statement.
- Banks and asset managers with off-balance-sheet cryptocurrencies: If these entities lose control over such cryptocurrencies, the customer liability must still be reported on the balance sheet if they bear the custody risk.

Crypto custody can significantly impact a company and its audit. Loss of control over digital assets may lead to asset write-downs and additional liabilities on the balance sheet, potentially resulting in insolvency and the need for restructuring.

7.3 Types of Crypto Custody Solutions

Securing private keys and backups is paramount, particularly by keeping them separate and safeguarded against internal and external threats. Professional crypto custody solutions play a critical role in mitigating risks related to confidentiality, availability, and integrity of private keys and backups throughout their life cycle.

Companies must decide on the type of crypto custody solution to implement, considering two key aspects:

1. Internal or external custody solution: Companies must decide whether to build an internal solution or engage an external provider. Internal solutions require building expertise, while external providers delegate custody tasks but still require oversight, especially regarding internal control systems.
2. Cold, warm, or hot storage solution: Distinctions exist between cold (offline), warm (combining features of cold and hot), and hot (online) storage solutions. Each has its advantages and trade-offs in terms of security and transaction speed.

These storage solutions typically utilize hardware security modules (HSMs) or multi-party computation (MPC) environments to protect private keys. Backups are usually stored in secure locations with trusted third parties.

7.4 Risks and Measures from an Auditor's Perspective

To mitigate risks, auditors should verify that robust controls are in place for safeguarding private keys and their backups throughout their life cycle. This is essential for preventing compromise and potential loss of digital assets.

Whether a company employs its own solution or outsources custody, auditors are responsible for assessing risks and testing controls. If an external provider offers a control report, auditors must carefully evaluate it and may need to audit complementary user entity controls.

Involving the auditor from the beginning, such as during the key ceremony, can help reduce potential risks. The auditor must verify secure storage of private keys and their backups and ensure that only authorized employees can initiate cryptocurrency sales.

Auditors should also assess the probability of digital asset loss and its impact on financial statements, particularly regarding the company's ability to continue as a going concern.

7.5 Conclusion

Private keys and their backups are crucial for accessing and controlling digital assets on the blockchain. Establishing effective control systems can mitigate risks related to the availability, confidentiality, and integrity of private keys and backups. Companies must act promptly to set up such systems, as loss of control over cryptocurrencies poses significant risks. Auditors play a vital role in addressing these risks through appropriate audit procedures, ensuring effective controls for secure storage of private keys and their backups throughout their life cycle.

8 Institutional Client Management

8.1 Investing in digital assets and their underlying technology.

Digital assets have been the talk of the town in recent years, but have faced a barrage of negative publicity due to questionable service providers. Despite this, they remain an intriguing investment opportunity. Financial intermediaries such as asset managers and family offices have the means to offer clients exposure to this asset class through various avenues. However, each approach demands careful attention to associated risks and regulatory requirements.

Investment Options and Exposure

One alternative to directly investing in digital assets is to invest in the underlying technology, particularly distributed ledger technology. This can be achieved by investing in companies active in the blockchain, crypto, or digital assets space. Investments can take the form of equity, debt, or mezzanine, or by acquiring tokens of the respective companies.

When investing in blockchain-based digital assets, investors and financial intermediaries can opt to hold digital assets directly (involving hosted or un-hosted wallets) or be exposed indirectly through financial instruments with digital assets as their underlying.

Direct holding offers the advantage of better reactivity to market movements and the ability to initiate transactions at all times. Indirect investments provide exposure to digital assets within traditional infrastructure without the need for direct holding. However, they come with their own set of challenges, such as lower liquidity, restricted trading hours, and additional fee layers.

Adhering to Regulatory Requirements

Financial intermediaries must navigate regulatory requirements when providing clients with access to digital assets. The type of regulatory requirements will depend on the intended use of digital assets, such as asset management, portfolio or transaction-related investment advice, or technical advisory services. The qualification of the concerned tokens also influences the regulatory requirements.

Adjustments may be necessary in terms of know-how, organizational regulations, policies, risk and compliance frameworks, contractual frameworks with clients, and insurance coverage. For cross-border services, compliance with local laws and regulations is essential.

Selecting Service Providers

When investing directly in digital assets, financial intermediaries must carefully evaluate service providers. Considerations include custodianship of acquired assets, access to digital assets (brokerage), and the level of security provided. Clients are increasingly seeking regulated financial institutions for custodianship of their digital assets.

In Conclusion

Despite the challenges, digital assets present an exciting investment opportunity. By staying informed and ensuring the best options are provided, financial intermediaries can guide their clients through the world of digital assets and potentially reap the rewards.

8.2 Methods of digital asset investment

Family offices (FOs) and high-net-worth individuals (HNWIs) have been diving into the world of digital assets, primarily through cryptocurrency exchanges and crypto-focused hedge funds. In the early days of the digital asset industry, peer-to-peer trading platforms and cryptocurrency exchanges were the go-to places for buying and selling digital assets. However, as the industry matures and garners institutional interest, investors now have a variety of avenues to gain digital asset exposure, including hedge funds, cryptocurrency exchange-traded products, and direct investment in digital asset service providers.

Some researches have revealed that the top three methods for family offices and HNWIs to gain digital asset exposure are centralized or decentralized cryptocurrency exchanges, cryptocurrency-focused hedge funds, and direct investment in digital asset service providers. In an interview with a family office executive, they expressed a preference for a diversified approach to gain broad exposure to all major growth drivers behind the digital asset economy. They also mentioned relying on their general partner relationships to make thematic, sector-specific bets.

In the midst of recent market turbulence, family offices and high-net-worth individuals (HNWIs) have taken a more cautious approach to managing risk by converting their digital asset holdings to stablecoins or market-neutral strategies. An interviewee from an external asset manager emphasized the critical importance of safeguarding the principal value of digital asset investments, especially during periods of volatility.

Market-neutral strategies have also gained traction among FOs and HNWIs, aiming to exploit inefficiencies in pricing across different digital assets. This strategy has become a popular alternative investment choice, offering exposure to digital assets and returns without the need to predict market direction.

The digital asset industry landscape is complex and multifaceted, providing FOs and HNWIs with numerous avenues to gain exposure to digital assets. The selection of digital asset service providers is influenced by various factors, including the team's track record, industry reputation, business model, compliance standards, and more.

The team behind the service provider and past track record play a crucial role in the decision-making process for family offices and HNWIs when choosing their digital asset service providers. This is followed by aligning investment mandates and industry reputation. In light of recent market volatility, robust risk management controls and operational transparency are also vital considerations for FOs and HNWIs when selecting their digital asset service providers. One family office interviewee highlighted the financial transparency of a digital asset service provider, including the source of yield in yield-generating products offered, as a crucial factor, particularly in light of recent market volatility.

FO and HNWIs place a premium on user experience and data security when it comes to selecting cryptocurrency exchanges. The cryptocurrency exchange landscape is highly diverse, with approximately 300 centralized exchanges and over 200 decentralized exchanges as of September 30, 2022. When evaluating a cryptocurrency exchange, factors to consider include trading volume, product offerings, liquidity, security, user experience, and more. A recent research reveals that 74 percent of respondents prioritize user-friendly cryptocurrency exchanges that deliver a positive user experience.

Additional influential factors in the selection of cryptocurrency exchanges include a demonstrated track record of security and regulatory compliance. One high-net-worth investor stressed that security outweighs the quantity of coin offerings when choosing cryptocurrency exchanges. He expressed confidence that exchanges with robust security measures are more likely to attract professional traders and are less susceptible to hacking.

Leading cryptocurrency exchanges cater to a wide range of customer segments across the wealth spectrum, each with varying levels of maturity, sophistication, and experience in dealing with digital platforms. A positive experience on cryptocurrency platforms extends beyond ease of use, with many platforms leading the industry in offering innovative propositions. For less experienced users, the focus is on simplicity, while more experienced users seek new and unique propositions. Consequently, cryptocurrency platforms often provide extensive education systems for these propositions to ensure a high-level experience. This includes providing videos to guide users and implementing appropriate risk management disclaimers.

8.3 Technological And Regulatory Developments will unleash Institutional blockchain adoption.

Consolidation of technological developments will shape the landscape. The crypto markets have seen continuous technological advancements aimed at overcoming key barriers to institutional blockchain adoption in financial markets. In 2023, innovations in interoperability solutions have facilitated the execution of increasingly complex institutional test cases across various private and public blockchains. The emergence of layer 2 roll-ups within the Ethereum ecosystem, particularly those utilizing zero knowledge proofs, shows promise in addressing scalability and privacy limitations, paving the way for potential institutional use cases.

Regulatory progress will be uneven despite collaborative efforts. The Financial Stability Board's publication of a global regulatory framework for crypto-asset activities in July offers high-level recommendations, but policy choices and timing are expected to vary significantly across jurisdictions. In the U.S., progress may be hindered by a fragmented regulatory framework and increasing political polarization, while regulatory frameworks in other regions are making strides, particularly in stablecoin regulation. For instance, the EU's Markets in Crypto-Assets (MiCA) will enforce stablecoin regulations from July 2024, with rules for other service providers following in January 2025. Additionally, the Monetary Authority of Singapore finalized a comparable regulation on stablecoins in August 2023.

Institutional testing of new use cases will gain momentum. Incumbent financial institutions are poised to further embrace blockchain technology to optimize processes or develop new tools for institutional users, supported by regulatory "sandbox" schemes in key jurisdictions. Notable examples include the trial launch of stablecoins or tokenized deposits by several banks across regions. Other institutional use cases encompass collateral mobility, foreign exchange, and cross-border payments. However, the commercialization of crypto assets to retail clients is expected to progress more slowly until regulatory frameworks offer greater clarity. Notably, a spot bitcoin exchange-traded fund (ETF) received regulatory approval in the EU in 2023, with several spot bitcoin and ether ETFs currently under review in the U.S.

The evolution and expansion of digital bond issuance is deemed credit neutral. Digital bonds aim to automate segments of fixed-income markets using blockchain technology, and while a small but growing universe of rated issuers are expected to experiment further with digital bonds, widespread acceptance of digital currencies and know-your-customer solutions is necessary for bonds to become fully digital and exchangeable on the blockchain. Regulatory pilot schemes will contain experimentation with fully digital bonds, limiting issuers' exposure to new operational and technological risks.

Regulated stablecoins will encourage experimentation by some rated issuers in financing real-world applications. The absence of central bank digital currencies (CBDCs) has thus far hindered the issuance of fully digital bonds and on-chain financing of fiat-denominated real-world assets. However, as regulatory frameworks for stablecoins come into play in 2024, the emergence of regulated stablecoins could address this issue. Real use cases at scale are expected to remain several years away, with ratings not likely to be affected by shifts in the competitive landscape in the near term.

The lines between centralized and decentralized finance (DeFi) will become increasingly blurred. As decentralized protocols emerge to provide financing to the real economy, some level of centralization will be necessary due to regulatory hurdles and accountability requirements when offering financial products. Regulators are beginning to focus on DeFi, aiming to strike a balance between investor protection and recognizing the unique features of DeFi. The development of regulatory frameworks should create opportunities for incumbent financial institutions to participate in innovative projects with decentralized elements. Meanwhile, centralized crypto businesses operating globally will need to comply with emerging regulatory frameworks in key jurisdictions. Competitive dynamics are not expected to significantly affect credit risk in 2024.

9 Emerging Trends in Digital Asset Custody

9.1 Emerging trends

In the realm of digital assets, an emerging and continually morphing landscape awaits. This nascent space, though still in its infancy, is no stranger to rapid evolution. The custodial domain, entrusted with the responsibility of safeguarding these digital treasures, stands at the forefront of this transformative tide.

As the digital asset arena navigates its early stages, it becomes evident that adaptability is not just a virtue but a necessity. The custodial landscape, akin to a vigilant guardian, must stay attuned to the pulse of innovation and the cadence of industry trends. In this dynamic environment, where change is not a question of if but when, custodians find themselves on the frontline, poised to embrace and respond to the ever-unfolding advancements.

The sensitivity of the custodial industry to technological innovation is paramount. With the expanding horizons of Bitcoin and Ethereum wallets serving as a compelling testament, a palpable trend emerges — one of burgeoning usage and widespread adoption. Custodians, akin to digital shepherds, are compelled to traverse the terrain of innovative shifts, ensuring that they not only keep pace but lead the charge in facilitating the institutionalization of digital assets.

In this landscape of perpetual evolution, custodians are tasked with more than safekeeping; they are the architects of a secure and responsive ecosystem. The narrative unfolds not as a mere chronicle of industry changes but as a call to custodians — urging them to be not only guardians of digital assets but pioneers in the orchestration of a harmonious integration between technology and institutional trust. The journey is not merely about responding to change; it is about envisioning the future and sculpting it with the chisel of adaptability and foresight.

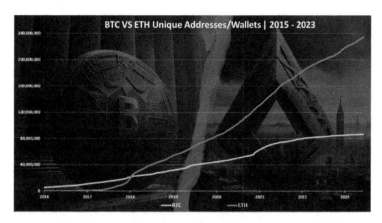

BTC vs ETH unique addresses

9.2 Staking

In the intricate tapestry of the digital asset realm, staking emerges as a pivotal mechanism, propelled by the widespread adoption of Layer 1 protocols employing Proof-of-Stake. Layer 1s, exemplified by tokens like ETH or SOL, orchestrate their own blockchain networks, ushering in a paradigm shift in consensus mechanisms.

A noteworthy revelation unfolds as the end of August bears witness to a staggering $20 billion securely staked in decentralized protocols. This robust figure underscores not only the substantial value but also the materialization of Total Value Locked (TVL) within the fabric of staking contracts. Yet, this is not merely a statistic; it serves as a precursor to an evolving landscape where staking services are poised to undergo a transformational embrace by institutional capital.

As the industry matures, a discernible trend emerges — an impending dominance of staking services by institutional players. In this maturation process, custodians stand as key architects, entrusted with the responsibility of facilitating a seamless transition. Their role extends beyond traditional safekeeping; it morphs into a strategic partnership to enable non-native investors to harness the full spectrum of opportunities embedded in network validation and yield generation.

The operational assistance rendered by custodians becomes a linchpin in ensuring not just participation but secure and informed participation in these dynamic ecosystems. The narrative transcends the present; it invites custodians to navigate the evolving currents of staking, not merely as facilitators but as stewards of a landscape where institutional and individual interests converge harmoniously for the benefit of the entire digital asset ecosystem.

9.3 Tokenisation and Real-World Assets (RWA)

In the dynamic landscape of digital assets, the emergence of tokenized assets stands as a transformative trend. The year 2023, in particular, has witnessed a meteoric rise in the Total Value Locked (TVL) within Real World Asset (RWA) protocols, marking a tenfold increase since the inception of the year. This surge in TVL underscores a seismic shift in investor behavior, as they increasingly leverage this technology on-chain to venture into alternative asset classes.

While still in its infancy, the concept of tokenization harbors boundless potential. Its applicability spans a diverse spectrum of assets, transcending traditional boundaries. Equities, fixed income instruments, real estate holdings, commodities, private market investments, carbon credits, and even the realms of art and media are ripe for tokenization. This transformative approach not only democratizes access to a myriad of asset classes but also introduces a new paradigm in liquidity and ownership.

Stablecoins, often regarded as the tokenization of the dollar, constitute a noteworthy manifestation of this trend. The application of tokenization principles to fiat currencies, particularly the dollar, has unleashed a wave of capital-efficient benefits, revolutionizing the very essence of transferring value. The fusion of stability and digitization has not only streamlined transactions but has also heralded a novel era where the traditional and the avant-garde coalesce seamlessly.

As tokenization continues to mature, its influence reverberates beyond the realms of speculation, embedding itself as a cornerstone of a more inclusive and fluid financial ecosystem. The journey from its nascent stages to widespread adoption is underway, promising a future where the concept of ownership extends beyond the tangible, and the investment landscape becomes a tapestry woven with digital threads of innovation.

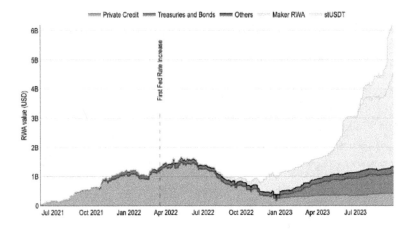

Coinbase: Tokenization and the new market cicle

In the expansive realm of finance, the trajectory of tokenization is set to soar exponentially, projecting an astronomic growth of over 80 times in private markets. The envisioned zenith, a staggering $4 trillion in value, is anticipated to be realized by the dawn of 2030 (Citi's GPS report). A parallel prophecy within this financial odyssey is the forecast that a substantial $1 trillion chunk of the repo, securities financing, and collateral market will undergo the transformative embrace of tokenization within the same temporal horizon.

In this unfolding saga, the custodian emerges as a pivotal character, wielding a crucial role in the theater of tokenization. The custodian's mantle, though dynamic and nuanced, hinges on the nature of assets under custody and the specific services engaged. Broadly delineated, the custodian shoulders a multi-faceted responsibility in the realm of tokenized assets.

- First and foremost, the custodian dons the hat of an asset manager. This entails deftly navigating the terrain of issuance, distribution, and redemption of tokenized assets on behalf of issuers or investors. Simultaneously, meticulous record-keeping of ownership is a pivotal facet of this custodial artistry.

- Liquidity enhancements form another dimension of the custodian's role. Serving as facilitators par excellence, custodians ensure seamless access to liquidity pools, thereby playing a vital role in facilitating the dynamic ebb and flow of tokenized asset transactions.

- Compliance and regulation stand as stalwart pillars of custodial responsibility. Custodians, as stewards of financial integrity, meticulously navigate the regulatory landscape, conducting necessary Know Your Customer (KYC) and Anti-Money Laundering (AML) measures to ensure unwavering compliance.

- The custodian's canvas extends further, encompassing the realm of security and transparency. Leveraging their robust security standards and on-chain expertise, custodians adeptly manage assets, offering a secure sanctuary while simultaneously upholding transparency and maintaining meticulous records.

It's noteworthy that, in many instances, tokenized assets find themselves tethered to the regulatory moorings of traditional finance. As they embark on the journey to the blockchain, investors are beckoned to entrust these regulated tokens to custodians, already seasoned in the art of regulatory adherence. A testament to this transition is the proactive stance adopted by some custodians, strategically implementing tokenization strategies. These custodians forge symbiotic partnerships with on-chain protocols issuing tokenized products, as well as traditional finance behemoths, crafting a bridge toward the promising expanse of on-chain assets.

9.4 DeFi & Interoperability

In the expansive realm of digital assets, the ascent of Decentralized Finance (DeFi) stands as a testament to exponential growth. DeFi, an avant-garde domain, unfurls a tapestry of possibilities, presenting a landscape where lending and borrowing transpire in a non-custodial ballet on the blockchain stage.

However, this remarkable trajectory is not devoid of shadows. The narrative of DeFi's ascent is interspersed with episodes of exploits, casting a pall over its meteoric rise. These exploits, akin to turbulent storms on the blockchain horizon, have introduced a nuanced layer of complexity, rendering institutional adoption a challenging endeavor. The associated risks, woven intricately into the fabric of these platforms, present a formidable barrier for institutions contemplating a direct embrace of these decentralized financial ecosystems.

As the DeFi saga unfolds, it echoes the dichotomy of promise and peril, where innovation burgeons against the backdrop of inherent challenges. The allure of a non-custodial financial frontier beckons, but the echoes of exploits underscore the imperative for the industry to navigate carefully through this uncharted territory.

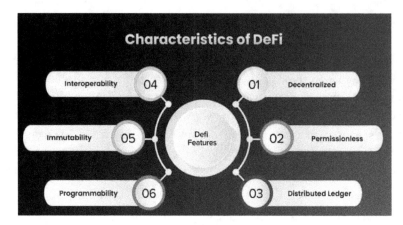

DeFi characteristics

Within the realm of digital assets, institutional custody providers emerge as custodians of a delicate balance, allowing institutions to partake in the enticing realm of DeFi protocols. This symbiotic dance between institutions and the dynamic landscape of decentralized finance not only promises opportunities and yields but also places a premium on the security and regulatory compliance of the assets involved.

In a strategic move to fortify this delicate equilibrium, custodians forge partnerships with select protocols, ushering institutions into the heart of DeFi right from the secure vantage point of their custody platforms. This innovative bridge, connecting the institutional stronghold with the decentralized expanse, encapsulates the essence of custodial prowess — offering direct and secure access while steadfastly maintaining the integrity of assets.

However, the DeFi narrative is not without its cautionary tales. Exploits, akin to lurking shadows, often find their stage on the vulnerabilities associated with bridges — pivotal mechanisms that enhance interoperability between diverse blockchains.

9.5 Institutional products

In this intricate tapestry, institutional products stand as resilient beacons. While the winds of retail investor participation may show signs of subsiding, marked by high derivatives-to-spot volume market shares (currently at 76%) and the consistent ebb of token prices favored by retail investors, a steadfast segment thrives: Digital Asset Exchange-Traded Products. This category, encompassing ETFs and Trusts, stands as a testament to enduring strength. Throughout the vicissitudes of the market, digital asset investment products maintain robust Assets Under Management (AUMs), standing tall with total aggregated AUMs exceeding a formidable $35 billion as of August 2023.

In the ever-evolving landscape of digital assets, seismic shifts reverberate through recent developments that underscore the maturation of institutional appetite. A pivotal moment materialized with the spot Bitcoin Exchange-Traded Fund (ETF) filing by a colossus of asset management, heralding an era where institutional investors are poised to engage with the space through meticulously regulated instruments.

While Futures ETFs have long provided a conduit for institutional traders to speculate on digital assets, the prospective approval of a Spot ETF in the United States looms as a paradigm-shifting moment for the sector. The trajectory of institutional sentiment has been buoyed by recent legal victories, notably in the Ripple camp. A judge's ruling affirming that XRP, when made available to the general public, does not classify as a security has monumental implications. This legal triumph not only augments the credibility of digital assets but also augurs a significant shift in their regulatory standing in the United States.

The resonance of this legal victory reverberates through the corridors of institutional accessibility. For institutions tethered by the regulatory purview of the U.S. Securities and Exchange Commission (SEC), the ruling expands the aperture, clearing the path for engagement with digital assets that may no longer be shackled by the securities classification.

As the legal landscape unfurls, a broader canvas emerges for the creation of innovative investment products. Altcoins, such as Solana, Ripple, and Cardano, stand poised at the nexus of this transformative wave. The legal wins not only embolden their standing but also pave the way for the conceptualization and realization of novel investment vehicles tailored around these emerging digital assets. The stage is set for institutional investors to not merely observe but actively participate in the burgeoning narrative of digital asset evolution.

9.6 Conclusions

The landscape of institutional involvement in digital assets is undergoing a dynamic transformation, necessitating custodians to be not just reactive but proactive in shaping their offerings. Central to this evolution is the persistent challenge of counterparty risk, a formidable barrier to entry that presents a ripe opportunity for custodians to galvanize adoption by effectively mitigating these risks for investment and asset managers.

In the quest for a custodial partner, institutions would be prudent to align with providers that manifest a commitment to innovation through cryptographic solutions. Exemplars in this realm, important custodians are leveraging cutting-edge technologies like Hardware Security Modules (HSM) or Order Execution Systems (OES). Embracing such services engenders a substantial reduction in counterparty risk, fostering a climate of confidence and safety for institutional entities navigating the complex digital asset terrain.

In the custodial arena, the deployment of insurance coverage and operational support emerges as a salient strategy. These multifaceted measures not only demystify the intricacies of engaging with an immutable distributed ledger but also furnish a safety net of recourse in times of exigency. Custodians, attuned to the evolving needs of their clientele, are diversifying their service portfolio. A notable trend is the expansion into tertiary services, especially those intertwined with trading. By facilitating trading via Application Programming Interface (API) through Over-the-Counter (OTC) and Prime Brokerage channels, custodians are strategically diminishing reliance on additional counterparties, each laden with its own inherent risk factors.

Nonetheless, this strategic shift necessitates custodians to tread with a keen awareness of the concomitant complexities and risks associated with their collaborators. A cautionary tale lies in the pitfalls observed in the lack of segregation of duties witnessed in pivotal centralized exchanges, a cautionary guidepost for custodians navigating this uncharted terrain.

Furthermore, as the digital asset ecosystem evolves, propelled by the expansive horizons of Decentralized Finance (DeFi) and the Tokenization of Real-World Assets (RWA), custodians poised to offer comprehensive coverage of these integral services stand as architects of the expected growth in these burgeoning sectors.

In tandem with the technological evolution is the crystallization of regulatory frameworks. With the advent of comprehensive virtual asset policies such as the Markets in Crypto Assets (MiCA), Financial Services Market Act (FSMA), and Virtual Asset and Virtual Asset Service Providers Act (VARA), the regulatory landscape is transitioning towards clarity. This, in turn, is poised to act as a catalyst for adoption by curtailing the regulatory risk associated with investing and building in this nascent space. As regulatory contours continue to metamorphose, institutions are well-advised to align with custodians demonstrating not just adaptability but a proactive embrace of these changes in a fluid and compliant manner.